Quality Management in Construction

QUALITY MANAGEMENT IN CONSTRUCTION

Brian Thorpe and Peter Sumner

GOWER

Published by
Gower Publishing Limited
Gower House
Croft Road
Aldershot
Hants GU11 3HR
England

Gower Publishing Company
Suite 420
101 Cherry Street
Burlington
VT 05401-4405
USA

Brian Thorpe and Peter Sumner have asserted their right under the Copyright, Designs and Patents Act, 1988 to be identified as the authors of this work.

British Library Cataloguing in Publication Data
Thorpe, Brian
 Quality management in construction. (The
 leading construction series)
 1. Construction industry – Great Britain – Quality control
 2. Construction industry – Great Britain – Management
 3. Quality assurance – Great Britain
 I. Title II. Sumner, Peter. III. Thorpe, Brian. Quality
 assurance in construction.
 624' .0685

 ISBN 0 566 08614 X

Library of Congress Cataloging-in-Publication Data
Thorpe, Brian.
 Quality management in construction / Brian Thorpe and Peter Sumner.
     p. cm. -- (Leading construction series)
 Rev. ed. of: Quality assurance in construction. 2nd ed. c.1996.
 ISBN 0-566-08614-X
 1. Engineering -- Great Britain -- Management. 2. Construction industry -- Great
Britain -- Quality control. 3. Quality assurance -- Great Britain. I. Sumner, Peter. II. Thorpe,
Brian. Quality assurance in construction. III. Title. IV. Series.

 TA190.T487 2004
 690'.0941--dc22

                                                                                    2004052266

Typeset by Secret Genius, 11 Mons Court, Winchester SO23 8GH.
Printed in Great Britain by MPG Books Ltd, Bodmin, Cornwall.

Contents

Chapter 1: Quality, Teams and Business Competition

Chapter 2 – ISO 9001:2000

Chapter 3 – Establishing a QMS

Chapter 10 – Monitoring Business/Process Effectiveness

Chapter 11 – Recognition of the QMS

Chapter 12 – Computers and Quality Management

Chapter 13 – The Future

Chapter 14 – Conclusions   211

List of Figures

List of Tables

List of Case Studies and Examples

ACOP	Approved Code of Practice
CAD	Computer-aided Design
CAP	corrective action programme
CDM Regulations	Construction (Design and Management) Regulations
COSHH	Control of Substances Hazardous to Health
DQP	detail quality plan
EFQM	European Foundation for Quality Management
FMEA	failure modes and effects analysis
HSE	Health and Safety Executive
ISO	International Standards Organization
KPI	key performance indicator
MOD	Ministry of Defence
MHSWR	Management of Health and Safety at Work Regulations
O & R	organization and responsibilities
PPE	personal protective equipment
PQP	project quality plan
QA	quality assurance
QMS	quality management system
RIBA	Royal Institute of British Architects
TQM	total quality management
UKAS	United Kingdom Accreditation Service

Since the second edition of this book (then entitled *Quality Assurance in Construction*) was published in 1996, the world of quality management has seen the continuing development of numerous good practices and business models, TQM (total quality management) and the EFQM (European Foundation for Quality Management) Excellence Model[TM] being two typical examples. Many organizations are aiming towards integrated management systems, incorporating safety and environmental factors.

To bring itself into line with current thinking the International Standards Organization introduced ISO 9001:2000, in which we find the term 'quality assurance' replaced by 'quality management', the 20 section headings of the previous ISO 9001:1994 regrouped under eight headings only, much greater emphasis on customer focus and satisfaction, processes highlighted as the key vehicles for achieving goals, plus an emphasis on the need for people to understand, participate and seek continual improvements in business processes and performance.

Many organizations that originally set up their quality management systems against ISO 9001:1994 have been updating (and, in many cases, continue to update) their systems against the expectations of the new standard. Others have still to start. At the same time, organizations continue to be confronted with new regulations and requirements, which ideally also need to be addressed through their quality management systems (QMSs). A significant example relating to the construction industry has been the Construction (Design and Management) Regulations 1994. Sadly, an HSE designer initiative held in Scotland and the north of England in March 2003 revealed that many designers were still unaware of their duties under CDM Regulation 13.

The ways in which we now do things, particularly communication, information storage and retrieval, have also significantly changed under the influences of continually emerging new information technology.

Yet, amidst all this apparent change perhaps we should pause and ask ourselves whether we are really looking at new things or merely at a repackaging of those common-sense things that we have known and practised with varying degrees of success for years. For example, what successful business remains unaware of the importance of:

- clearly establishing the expectations of its customers
- recognizing other stakeholders in its actions – for example, shareholders, staff and the public
- planning and using its resources in the most effective and efficient ways, in order to meet fully (or exceed) the expectations of those it serves
- establishing clearly defined processes, interfaces and responsibilities that are understood and accepted by all
- realizing the importance of its greatest asset – namely, its people – and of creating an environment in which they are able to contribute both individually and collectively to the improvement of its processes and business performance
- monitoring performance and customer satisfaction on an ongoing basis
- seeking continuing improvement.

These are essentially all that the latest standard ISO 9001:2000 asks of us.

What *is* new are the ways of accomplishing these basics – namely, the methodology and technology. In this book we attempt to demystify matters and look at ways in which you may address the basics of quality management through a quality management system, established, designed by and right for you.

The presentation style of the book is slightly different from that of earlier editions, with the view to making it both a useful training vehicle for those coming to the subject of quality management in construction for the first time, as well as an important reference for the industry as a whole.

We have presented the information in a logical sequence, reflecting what we believe to be a common-sense approach to the subject, based on our joint experiences of more than 50 years in the quality management field. We hope that you will find much of benefit within the following pages and wish you every success with your quality management system.

Brian Thorpe and Peter Sumner
2004

Chapter 1

Quality, Teams and Business Competition

Business success in a competitive environment

Whether we like it or not, we cannot ignore the fact that we live in a competitive environment. If we are in business and having to compete for market share, it will not be long before it becomes clear that survival and success are largely dependent on just a few very fundamental issues:

1　We have to be able to win the business in the first place – that is, convince potential customers that, given the opportunity, we can provide exactly what they want, better than anybody else. In this respect, anything that may give us a slight competitive edge is vital.

2　Having won the business, we must practise what we preach and meet fully (or exceed) the expectations of our customers, thereby giving them satisfaction and improving our prospects of further business.

Always remember that the testimony of a satisfied client/ customer is the best publicity we can have for our product(s) or service(s). In this context the philosophy 'If satisfied, tell others; if not, tell us' is a good one to aim for.

3　It is not enough to win business and consistently deliver satisfactory results; we also need to do this in ways which will simultaneously enable us to achieve our own business objectives – for example, profitability, return on investment/capital employed, satisfying our stakeholders and so on.

A key benefit of a quality management system is ensuring consistency and quality of service for your customers.

What, then, can a quality management system do to help us? One thing is certain: if such a system does not help us achieve these goals, we can well do without it. So, let us now look at what exactly a quality management system (QMS) is and how it works.

The QMS and its significance for business performance

What do we mean by 'quality'?

The word 'quality' appears just about everywhere, Quality Street® confectionery and 'Quality Used Car' being just two everyday examples.

However, if you ask people what 'quality' means to them, you will get a wide range of answers, such as 'the best' or 'fit for purpose', both of which beg further questions such as 'What constitutes the *best*?' or 'What exactly is the *purpose*?' and 'How is *fitness* to be judged?' Quality is subjective. What satisfies one person may fail to satisfy another. We define quality as:

Meeting fully (or exceeding) the expectations of those to whom you are providing a product or service.

This definition is useful because it embraces the internal customer (that is, the person who receives your output) as well as the external one.

What, then, is a QMS?

Our description is as follows:

A formal statement of an organization's business policy, management responsibilities, processes and their controls, that reflects the most effective and efficient ways to meet (or exceed) the expectations of those it serves, whilst achieving its own prime business objectives.

The following extract from Brian Thorpe's book *Addressing CDM Regulations through Quality Management Systems* (Aldershot: Gower, 1999) lists some of the key fundamentals that constitute a good QMS. It:

Remember, it is people, not systems who make things happen.

- enables us to identify with and completely meet our customers' needs.
- simultaneously enhances the achievement of our own prime business objectives.
- enjoys real management commitment and is based upon a clear policy, measurable objectives, strategy for quality attainment that is management led and supported at every level.
- is expressed in the most user-friendly way possible and is at any moment in time representative of the most effective and efficient ways we can devise for carrying out our business processes and their various discrete activities.
- clearly defines responsibilities for carrying out defined functions and activities.
- has been created with the participation and input of those who operate the system and, as such, is successful because of people's understanding of, commitment to and sense of ownership of it. (Remember systems alone do not cause things to happen – people do.)
- is dynamic, is seen as such and encourages inputs for improvements at any time from any source.
- recognizes the sound advice offered by standards such as ISO 9001:2000 insofar as they relate to one's particular business activities.
- includes techniques which enable the QMS to be used in a manner which is sensible, selective and cost effective; in other words to the degree commensurate with the real needs of the task.
- is formally and continuingly reviewed in a quest for ongoing improvements.
- provides visibility of one's capability to others, without unnecessarily disclosing information which is confidential.

A little later in this book we will describe how to set up a QMS to meet these criteria.

Winning business

For many years there has been a growing tendency for organizations placing contracts with, or seeking the support of, other firms to request evidence of an appropriate quality management capability. For many organizations this is one of the qualifying requirements for inclusion on their 'preferred supplier' lists. This will be particularly likely if the selecting organization itself operates a formal QMS, set up to satisfy the expectations of a quality standard such as ISO 9001:2000. This request for evidence of a QMS is nothing more than common sense. Why should someone who is about to place a significant order not be entitled to ask you what systems you have in place to ensure that their requirements will be properly established and agreed, and that a right result will be achieved on time and to budget? The ability to demonstrate that you have a recognized QMS is one way of confirming your capability to fulfil your customer's needs and can also be an important factor in winning business from sectors of the market or particular customers who may otherwise be debarred to you. How we can use our QMS capabilities to enhance our competitive edge is discussed later in Chapter 9 of this book.

Your QMS is the vehicle which defines your organization's agreed best ways of clearly establishing and confirming its customer needs and then selecting and managing the necessary processes, resources and activities in the most effective way to ensure the prospects of a correct, cost-effective and timely result.

Of course, setting up a QMS costs money and how it is done is all-important. If your system ultimately represents the most effective and efficient ways of doing things (in other words, it does the right things and does them correctly) and it is applied selectively and appropriately to achieve a particular result, then, by definition, *any* other way will be more costly. Your QMS and how it is used is the route to consistently satisfying your customers and simultaneously achieving your own prime business objectives. It is not an 'add on' to your other business systems, *it is* the management system of the business.

Teams and their value

Throughout this book we advocate teamworking in relation to a number of completely different situations.

Besides the advantages of a collective team approach in specific situations, teamworking can offer many significant benefits to those participating.

For example, teamworking:

- expands people's awareness of the subject under discussion
- provides an opportunity to learn and benefit from the knowledge and experience of others
- gives a greater appreciation of the roles and relative importance of others and their work
- offers an opportunity to contribute to the group decision-making process
- gives personal satisfaction from having contributed to collective achievement
- provides an opportunity to improve confidence and communication skills
- provides an opportunity to widen an individual's personal image and reputation
- engenders a sense of commitment to, and ownership of, the final decision because everyone is involved.

The TQM philosophy which we discuss briefly in the next section relies heavily on teamworking as a vehicle for gathering and developing information.

Try the following exercise. Bring together a small team (say six to eight people) of experienced construction design and project management personnel and then ask each to write down a list of points, independently and without discussion, which they feel should *always* be taken into consideration from a health and safety perspective, when designing a structure. Allow a limited time for this exercise – say, 15 minutes.

At the end of the allocated time, collect the lists and discuss them. Almost certainly there will be a number of factors common to all the lists, all of which can be agreed and recorded. However, there will also be a number of other factors which will have been listed by only a limited number of individuals or be unique to one person. These are likely to be reflections of individual knowledge or personal experiences. Discuss these factors and if the group accepts them as real points for design consideration, then they too can be recorded. The end result will almost inevitably be a bigger list than that produced by any single participating individual. Furthermore, it will be a list that will have been democratically arrived at and accepted by all involved as an improved basis for future designs.

The design team can benefit from contractor feedback – from people who understand the implications of decisions made on site.

What you have just done, with very little effort, is unlock the collective knowledge and experience of the group. Imagine, then, the benefits of extending the approach for identifying potential solutions if the team were to include contractor personnel (that is, the downstream customers/receivers of much of the design output) with their real-time knowledge of on-site implications.

Such mutually beneficial liaisons *are* possible. They will help break down perceptions of 'them' and 'us', promote the spirit of project cooperation and, hopefully, go a long way towards addressing the problems identified in the HSE designer initiative survey, mentioned in the Preface to this book.

Total quality management and the TQM/QMS relationship

The TQM approach

During recent years many organizations have moved significantly away from an autocratic style of management towards a more democratic approach, recognizing that the greatest asset of any business is the people who work within it, particularly the doers/value-adders whose close knowledge of process strengths and weaknesses gained at the 'coal face' is second to none.

[If you can create, within your organization, a culture and environment which both encourages and enables the individual and collective participation of everybody in improving your business processes, then a huge potential will have been released for the benefit of your business and those involved in it. This is the TQM approach.]

The change from a traditional style 'top-down' autocratic management structure to one which enables greater participation by, and empowerment of, non-management personnel cannot be achieved overnight. In fact, in some organizations certain managers may be reluctant to relinquish control (as they see it) by empowering others to become involved in the collective decision-making role. This is unfortunate. If we can accept that the definition of a manager is 'someone who achieves results through others', then the TQM approach does not represent a dilution of a manager's responsibilities, but essentially a change to a more facilitating role, encouraging, guiding and enabling.

The main thrust of TQM is continuing improvement, enhanced competitive edge and business performance.

If you don't record improvements, how will you remember and share them?

In the early days of TQM many organizations, eager to benefit from the approach, rushed to apply the techniques before they had a QMS in place. Consequently, although improvements were identified with regard to the ways of doing things, there was no vehicle in which they could be recorded and become the accepted norm for the benefit of others. As a result, in some organizations quality management got a bad name, which then made the task (which should have happened first) of setting up a QMS, which depends on the cooperation of all concerned, far more difficult than it should have been.

We recommend you start by establishing a QMS. When appropriate, TQM techniques are used to achieve this objective and to familiarize people with the benefits of such concepts as teamworking.

Figure 1.1 shows the TQM/QMS relationship in simple terms.

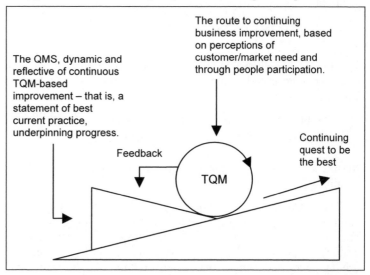

The route to continuing business improvement, based on perceptions of customer/market need and through people participation.

The QMS, dynamic and reflective of continuous TQM-based improvement – that is, a statement of best current practice, underpinning progress.

Continuing quest to be the best

Feedback

TQM

Figure 1.1 *Simple diagram illustrating the TQM/QMS interface*

The EFQM Excellence Model™

History and background

In 1988 the presidents of 14 major European companies founded EFQM. The impetus was to develop a European framework along the lines of the Malcolm Baldridge Model in the USA and the Deming Prize in Japan. Both these awards have demonstrably improved service and manufacturing quality in the organizations that used them.

The European Model for Business Excellence – now called the EFQM Excellence Model™ was introduced in 1991 as the framework for organizational self-assessment and as the basis of judging entrants to the European Quality Award, which was awarded for the first time in 1992.

From the outset EFQM has been aimed at helping organizations in Europe that practise the principals of TQM in the way they do business.

The true measure of the EFQM Excellence Model's™ effectiveness lies in its use as a management tool and the associated growth in the management discipline of organizational 'self-assessment'.

Regardless of the size, structure or market sector of an organization, the EFQM Excellence Model™ can be used as a tool to help organizations to establish or improve their management systems. It does this by measuring where they are on the path to 'excellence', helping them understand the gaps and then stimulating solutions.

Overview of the EFQM Excellence Model™

The EFQM Excellence Model™ is a non-prescriptive framework based on nine criteria, five of which are 'enablers' and four of which are 'results'.

- **Enablers** cover what the organization does.
- **Results** cover what an organization achieves.

Results are caused by 'enablers' and feedback from 'results' helps to improve 'enablers'.

The EFQM Excellence Model™ recognizes that there are many approaches to achieving sustainable excellence and it is based on the premise that excellent results with respect to performance, customers, people and society are achieved through leadership driving policy and strategy that is delivered through the partnership of people, resources and processes (see Figure 1.2). This statement could equally describe a QMS.

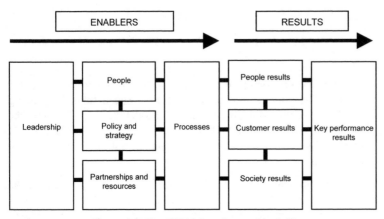

Figure 1.2 *The EFQM Excellence Model™*

Each of the nine criteria carries a points rating. Through the use of in-depth questionnaires, self-audit techniques and benchmarking, a score can be determined indicating where the gaps are and where scope exists for further improvement.

Details regarding the model's nine criteria against which to assess an organization can be found on the EFQM website: <www.efqm.org>.

Chapter 2

ISO 9001:2000

The background to quality standards

As can be seen from Figure 2.1, the current English-language version of the international quality standard operating in the UK is BS EN ISO 9001:2000 – Quality Management Systems – Requirements. The British Standard is the official English-language version of EN ISO 9001:2000 and is identical with ISO 9001:2000. Hereafter we will refer to ISO 9001:2000.

This is not a sector-specific standard, but one that applies equally to the construction industry, the wider engineering industry and the service sector.

It is assumed that you will be in possession of a copy of ISO 9001:2000 – Quality Management Systems – Requirements.

Principal expectations

The main thrusts of the ISO 9001:2000 standard are:

- the adoption of a 'process approach' as opposed to having activities based on departments
- process ownership with measurable outputs that can be judged in terms of effectiveness
- extra emphasis on management commitment
- extra emphasis on continuous improvement
- a change of terminology regarding organization, customer, supplier and so on
- the removal of the term 'quality assurance' in favour of 'quality management'
- the re-categorization of the 20 elements of the 1994 standard into eight sections in the 2000 standard
- the reflection of trends, such as TQM
- only six mandatory procedures with more flexibility – that is, taking into account that the professionalism, experience, qualifications and so on of the workforce are identified within ISO 9001:2000. Most organizations, however, will feel that they will need more than the six listed procedures (see below), particularly if they have become comfortable working with management systems set up against ISO 9001:1994.

Most of the requirements of the ISO 9001:1994 have been picked up by the ISO 9001:2000 standard as can be seen from the comparison chart in Table 2.1. This chart has been included for the particular benefit of those currently updating their management systems, or planning to do so.

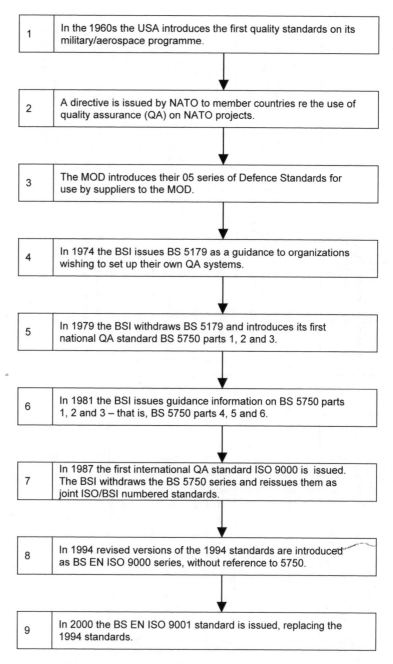

1	In the 1960s the USA introduces the first quality standards on its military/aerospace programme.
2	A directive is issued by NATO to member countries re the use of quality assurance (QA) on NATO projects.
3	The MOD introduces their 05 series of Defence Standards for use by suppliers to the MOD.
4	In 1974 the BSI issues BS 5179 as a guidance to organizations wishing to set up their own QA systems.
5	In 1979 the BSI withdraws BS 5179 and introduces its first national QA standard BS 5750 parts 1, 2 and 3.
6	In 1981 the BSI issues guidance information on BS 5750 parts 1, 2 and 3 – that is, BS 5750 parts 4, 5 and 6.
7	In 1987 the first international QA standard ISO 9000 is issued. The BSI withdraws the BS 5750 series and reissues them as joint ISO/BSI numbered standards.
8	In 1994 revised versions of the 1994 standards are introduced as BS EN ISO 9000 series, without reference to 5750.
9	In 2000 the BS EN ISO 9001 standard is issued, replacing the 1994 standards.

Figure 2.1 *Brief history of quality standards used in the UK*

ISO 9001:2000	ISO 9001:1994	Changes from ISO 9001:1994 to ISO 9001:2000
1 Scope	1 Scope	
1.1 General		
1.2 Application		A single, more generic standard than previously. Those organizations with a current ISO 9002 or ISO 9003 certification need to state those requirements of clause 7 that do not apply.
2 Normative references	2 Normative reference	Revised terminology needs to be considered.
3 Terms and Definitions	3 Definitions	Revised terminology – that is, product also now means *service*. *Organization* is used as a replacement for *supplier*. *Supplier* is used as a replacement for *subcontractor*.
4 Quality management system		New heading.
4.1 General requirements	4.2.1 (Quality system) General	This defines the starting point for planning and setting up the QMS, to identify processes needed for the QMS, determine criteria and methods to ensure the effective operation of processes.
4.2 Documentation requirements	4.2.2 Quality system procedures	Major change of approach to implementation. A correct balance is needed between the amount of documentation and the competence of personnel required for achieving the requirements.
4.2.1 General	4.2.2 Quality system procedures	There is no requirement for any particular format for documentation. The change of emphasis results in only six documented procedures being obligatory.
4.2.2 Quality Manual	4.2.1 (Quality system) General	The requirement is not new although there now has to be details of the justification for excluding clause 7.
4.2.3 Control of documents	4.5.2 Document and data approval and issue; 4.5.3 Document and data changes	Little change, although documents to be controlled need to be identified.

4.2.4 Control of records	4.16 Control of quality records	A review of records should be undertaken to ensure all the requirements of ISO 9001:2000 are addressed (see pages 18–19 for more detail of records required).
5 Management responsibility		New heading.
5.1 Management commitment	4.1.1 Quality policy	More emphasis on top management to demonstrate commitment to develop and improve the QMS, and have evidence to show results.
5.2 Customer focus	4.3.2 Review	Requirement for top management to ensure customer needs and expectations are determined and requirements are fulfilled. Greater visibility required.
5.3 Quality policy	4.1.1 Quality policy	More realistic defined quality policy required, which is achievable. This policy has to be periodically reviewed.
5.4 Planning		
5.4.1 Quality objectives	4.1.1 Quality policy	New requirement for quality objectives to be more specific and relate to the processes, and be measurable.
5.4.2 Quality management system planning	4.2.3 Quality planning	Emphasis on high-level planning of the QMS and tangible outputs.
5.5 Responsibility, authority and communication		New title and the requirement for 'effective communication' of the QMS.
5.5.1 Responsibility and authority	4.1.2.1 Responsibility and authority	Roles and authorities have to be documented and communicated.
5.5.2 Management representative	4.1.2.3 Management representative	Requirement for the management representative to promote awareness of customer requirements.
5.5.3 Internal communication		New requirement to ensure that the approach to effective communications is planned and seen to be working at levels and functions.
5.6 Management review		

Table 2.1 Analysis of ISO 9001:2000 (continued)

ISO 9001:2000	ISO 9001:1994	Changes from ISO 9001:1994 to ISO 9001:2000
5.6.1 General	4.1.3 3 Management review	Management reviews to be a key driver for improvement to the QMS, quality policy and quality objectives. More proactive approach required.
5.6.2 Review input	4.1.3 Management review	Records of inputs to management review to be identified.
5.6.3 Review output	4.1.3 Management review	Records of outputs from management review to be identified.
6 Resource management		
6.1 Provision of resources	4.1.2.2 Resources	Sufficient resources required to improve processes relating to the QMS and address customer satisfaction. Resources now includes infrastructure such as buildings.
6.2 Human resources		New heading rather than a new requirement.
6.2.1 General	4.1.2.2 Resources	Requirement that personnel-assigned responsibilities shall be competent. Evidence of reviewing performance and skills now required.
6.2.2 Competence, awareness and training	4.18 Training	New requirements to identify competency needs to ensure employee awareness of their activities and how they contribute to achieving quality objectives, and to maintain records of experience.
6.3 Infrastructure	4.9 Process control	Enhanced requirement to identify, provide and maintain workspace and support services.
6.4 Work environment	4.9 Process control	New requirement to identify critical work and impact on product quality by environmental issues – for example, temperature control, hygiene and contamination.
7 Product realization		New heading.
7.1 Planning of product realization	4.2.3 Quality planning; 4.10 Inspection and testing	Revised requirement for an organization to review its arrangements for planning the processes to meet customer and regulatory requirements.
7.2 Customer-related processes		New heading.

7.2.1 Determination of requirements related to the	4.3.2 Review; 4.4.4 Design input	Revised requirements to review existing arrangements for determining customer, product and legal requirements related to the product.
7.2.2 Review of requirements related to the product	4.3 2 Review; 4.3.3 Amendment to a contract; 4.3.4 Records	This revised requirements can be applied by a contract review, prior to offering to supply, as in the case of catalogue or Internet-based sales.
7.2.3 Customer communication	4.3.2 Review	New requirements to review the effectiveness of current communications with customers on products, enquiries and feedback.
7.3 Design and development		
7.3.1 Design and development planning	4.4.2 Design and development planning; 4.4.3 Organizational and technical interfaces	Revised emphasis is on planning rather than plans, whether it is a service or a product that is being designed.
7.3.2 Design and development inputs	4.4.4 Design input	Revised design inputs identified: functional and performance requirements in addition to information from previous designs and other references.
7.3.3 Design and development outputs	4.4.5 Design output	Revised requirements for design outputs to provide information for production and servicing and to be approved prior to release.
7.3.4 Design and development review	4.4.6 Design review	Revised requirement for review to evaluate ability to fulfil requirements in addition to identifying and resolving problems.
7.3.5 Design and development verification	4.4.7 Design verification	Design verification activities have to be planned to ensure that outputs have met the input requirements.
7.3.6 Design and development validation	4.4.8 Design validation	New requirements for validation to be completed (wherever applicable) prior to delivery and implementation, and for results of validation and any necessary actions to be maintained.
7.3.7 Control of design and development changes	4.4.9 Design changes	New requirements for design changes to be reviewed, verified and validated as appropriate before implementation.
7.4 Purchasing		4.6.2 Evaluation of suppliers.
7.4.1 Purchasing process	4.6.2 Evaluation of subcontractors	More specific requirement for the periodic re-evaluation of suppliers.
7.4.2 Purchasing information	4.6.3 Purchasing data	

Table 2.1 Continued

ISO 9001:2000	ISO 9001:1994	Changes from ISO 9001:1994 to ISO 9001:2000
7.4.3 Verification of purchased products	4.6.4 Verification of purchased product	Simplified requirements. No change but emphasizes that the organization must identify its intentions regarding verification in its purchasing documents.
7.5 Production and service provision		New heading.
7.5.1 Control of production and service provision	4.9 Process control, 4.15.6 Delivery; 4.19 Servicing	Simplified list of requirements that are more generic in nature and capable of being interpreted and applied to any market sector.
7.5.2 Validation of processes for production and service provision	4.9 Process control	New requirement to identify 'process validation' rather than 'qualification of process operations'. Also less prescriptive regarding the types of control adopted.
7.5.3 Identification and traceability	4.8 Product Identification and traceability; 10.5 Inspection and test records; 4.12 Inspection and test status	Customer property may include intellectual property. The organization should review its current processes for identification and traceability.
7.5.4 Customer property	4.7 Control of customer supplied product	The significant change is that the customer property requirements relate to all customer property that is used by the organization, including the fabric of the customer's premises and the customer's intellectual property.
7.5.5 Preservation of product	4.15.2 Handling; 4.15.3 Storage; 4.15.4 Packaging; 4.15.4 Preservation	It should be noted that ISO 9001:2000, 6.3 is relevant to this clause for the provision of any required facilities.
7.6 Control of monitoring and measuring devices	4.11 Control of inspection, measuring and test equipment	No additional requirements, but the requirements are presented in a manner that should encourage organizations to re-examine their control of measuring and test equipment.
8 Measurement, analysis and improvement		New heading.
8.1 General	4.10 Inspection and testing: 4.20 Statistical techniques	Greater emphasis on planning in this standard should lead to a more integrated approach to measurement, monitoring, analysis and improvement.

8.2 Monitoring and measurement		New heading.
8.2.1 Customer satisfaction		New requirement to establish what information is available and what is needed on customer satisfaction/dissatisfaction. Information is to be monitored and analysed.
8.2.2 Internal audit	4.17 Internal quality audits	The reason for audits is now to determine whether the QMS has been effectively implemented and maintained in supporting the quality policy and objectives.
8.2.3 Monitoring and measurement of processes	4.17 Internal quality audit; 4.20 Statistical techniques	An organization must identify all its QMS processes and monitor them.
8.2.4 Monitoring and measurement of product	4.10 Inspection and testing; 4.20 Statistical techniques	Simplified version of previous requirements – more generic and can be applied to the service sector.
8.3 Control of non-conforming product	4.13 Control of non-conforming product	More generic requirements. New requirement for action if non-conformity is detected after delivery or use has started.
8.4 Analysis of data	4.14 Corrective and preventive action; 4.20 Statistical techniques	New requirement to collect and analyse data to determine suitability and effectiveness of QMS and to identify improvements. Requirement to focus on important characteristics related to customer requirements, processes and suppliers, as well as areas where quality objectives have been set.
8.5 Improvement		New heading.
8.5.1 Continual improvement	4.1.3 Management review process	New requirement for the organization to focus on those aspects that the customer considers important as well as areas where quality objectives have been set.
8.5.2 Corrective action	4.14 Corrective and preventive action	No significant change.
8.5.3 Preventive action	4.14 Corrective and preventive action	No significant change.

Table 2.1 Concluded

The relationship to the previous standard ISO 9001:1994

Table 2.1 documents the changes that have taken place as a result of the move from the ISO 9001:1994 standard to the current ISO 9001:2000 standard. However, there is more to consider when setting up a quality management system to ISO 9001:2000 or if reviewing an existing QMS which has not yet been updated to meet the current standard – namely:

- documented procedures
- other specific requirements for documents
- specific requirements for records.

Documented procedures are required as follows:

Clause	Requirement
4.2.3	Control of documents
4.2.4	Control of quality records
8.2.2	Internal audit
8.3	Control of non-conforming product
8.5.2	Corrective action
8.5.3	Preventive action

Other specific requirements for documents are as follows:

Clause	Requirement
4.1	A quality management system
4.2.1	Documents required to ensure effective operation and control of processes
5.4.2	The output of quality planning
5.5.5	Quality manual
7.1	Planning of product realization processes
7.3.2	Inputs relating to product requirements
7.3.3	Outputs of the design and/or development process
7.3.7	Design and/or development changes
7.3.7	Results of the review of (design) changes and subsequent follow-up actions
7.4.2	Purchasing documents
8.2.4	Evidence of conformity with acceptance criteria

Specific requirements for records are as follows:

Clause	Requirement
5.6.1	Management reviews
6.2.2	Education, experience, training and qualifications
7.1	Evidence that realization processes and resultant products meet requirements
7.2.2	Results of review of product requirements and subsequent follow-up actions

7.3.4	Results of design and/or development reviews and subsequent follow-up actions
7.3.5	Results of design and/or development verification and subsequent follow-up actions
7.3.6	Results of design and/or development validation and subsequent follow-up actions
7.4.1	Results of supplier evaluations and follow-up actions
7.5.3	The unique identification of product, where traceability is a requirement
7.5.4	Any occurrence of customer property being lost, damaged or unsuitable for use
7.6	The basis of calibration where no international or national standards exist
7.6	The results of calibration
8.2.2	Results of internal audit
8.2.4	Authority responsible for release of product
8.5.2	Results of corrective action taken
8.5.3	Results of preventive action taken

Quality standards in the construction industry: detailed analysis

Since 1979, mainly due initially to the requirements on nuclear power stations, the construction industry has gradually adopted the QMS approach.

With the advent of the latest quality management standard ISO 9001:2000, those in the construction industry, like organizations in other sectors, have had to revisit their current quality management systems to see what changes are required to satisfy this standard. As a result, many construction organizations have now converted their QMSs to meet the requirements of ISO 9001:2000. It can be seen from Table 2.1 that there are some significant changes to the standard, and these have involved making fundamental changes to their QMSs. Some organizations view this process in terms of making costly changes to the way in which they operate; others (those who can see the value-added benefits of implementing the standard) look on it as a way of improving their business.

We now take a look at some of the questions raised by construction companies relating to clauses of the new standard and see how they can be addressed.

Clause 5.4.1 Quality objectives

What sorts of quality objectives are appropriate?

It is the responsibility of top management to identify and establish measurable quality objectives and use them as a means of leading the organization towards improved performance. These quality objectives must be achievable and relevant to the organization's needs and consistent with the quality policy.

Quality objectives can identify both corporate quality issues and local issues. Typical objectives for a contractor could be:

- response time to customer queries, design change requests and so on
- delivery on time and to budget
- reduction in accidents
- reduction in internal failures or rework.

As can be seen from the above list, these quality objectives relate to both processes and products.

Quality objectives should give 'added value' and therefore it is important that the people most likely to be providing input information and be affected should be involved in their initial identification. This will go a long way towards their general acceptance.

If you want your quality objectives to be meaningful, make sure you involve the appropriate people in drawing them up.

How can quality objectives be communicated and implemented?

It is pointless identifying quality objectives if they are not deployed and communicated throughout the organization (see ISO 9001:2000, 6.2.2). Therefore a prerequisite is to:

- brief all staff in order to cascade down the quality objectives
- identify timescales to achieve agreed targets
- have suitable indicators to measure against – for example, key performance indicators (KPIs).

Don't have too many objectives and targets or people will spend all of their time collecting and gathering data without adding value.

It is important that individual managers are identified to collect data in a consistent format and at regular intervals, feed the data back to a nominated person to collate, and then communicate the results in a timely manner.

Clause 8.2.1   Customer satisfaction

How do we gather information on customers' views thus giving a measure of QMS performance?

Obtaining customer feedback is perceived by many contractors as a problem. How can customer satisfaction be measured?

The most obvious sign of satisfied customers is repeat business.

One obvious measure of customer satisfaction is the number of repeat orders. However, this is not a very scientific way of measuring your organization's performance. What is required is an approach that encompasses:

- measurement
- analysis
- improvement.

Before we can do the above we need data. The cornerstone of this sort of approach is data.

Collecting and analysing data

The standard requires organizations to gather data, typical input data being:

- feedback reports from sales staff
- complaints
- cancelled work
- warranty claims
- inspection and audit reports from customers
- market surveys.

These inputs should enable your organization to evaluate both satisfaction and dissatisfaction.

The first step is to establish what information is already available and whether it is in a form that can be used in this process. You will probably find that more data is needed, so you will then need to put into place methods of gathering information if you do not already have them. The amount of data you need to collect very much depends on the size and complexity of your organization. If you are a small contractor with a few customers you can measure customer satisfaction on the basis of a simple customer questionnaire used at defined frequencies.

The next step is to establish responsibilities for collecting and analysing data and agree the method of reporting the information and using it for measuring trends over a period of time.

Using data for improvement

Once you have analysed the data you can then use it to:
- give a customer perception of the degree to which your products or services are meeting expectations
- identify areas for improvement
- feed back into management reviews and ultimately to improvements in the QMS.

Clause 8.5.3   Preventive action

How do we implement a procedure for preventive action?

There is very little guidance in the standard as to what should be in this procedure, although this is one of the six mandatory procedures demanded in ISO 9001:2000. You need to look at why this issue has been given prominence and why it demands a formal documented procedure.

What are we preventing?

Like all organizations, your company is subject to potential risks and potential non-conformances, which could affect its ability to supply its products and services on time and in accordance with the customer's expectations.

Preventive action is one of the key contributors to continual improvement and links in with other parts of our QMS, such as clause 7.2.2, Contract Review, and clause 5.6, Management Review.

Identifying what to prevent

When organizations set up their processes they need to look at the risks of things going wrong. This list could be endless, but let us consider some typical risks and their consequences and rank them in some sort of order of importance. The following is a typical list of risks:

1   risks to the building fabric and its contents – for example, security of tenure, fire, flood, theft, equipments and so on
2   risks in developing new products, processes, materials and services, and bringing them to the market
3   changes in the marketplace as a result of inflation, wars, fashion and so on
4   accidents in the workplace
5   technical risks of things going wrong as a result of faults with the design, faults in materials and faults in workmanship
6   risks to the business resulting from competition, loss of customers, lawsuits, key staff leaving or failure of the IT systems.

What are the most likely
risks to your business and
which of them would do
the most harm?

How do we take preventive action?

Looking at the above, you should ask yourself what potential harm each could cause to your business and what steps you can take to prevent an occurrence.

1 **Risks to the building fabric and its contents**. These risks can be planned for. You can have insurance in place and negotiate a long-term lease. Planned maintenance is one way of preventing things going wrong and is advocated as a cost-effective strategy to ensure that the building and any equipment are kept in a good state of repair. The maintenance procedure will be contained in the QMS.

2 **Risks in developing new products, processes, materials and services, and bringing them to the market**. All development is going to cost money and resources. There has to be a balance between satisfying existing customers and contracts and carrying out research and development. There are risk assessment tools and risk reduction techniques that can be used, and these will be described in the QMS. The process may be titled 'Business Risk' and include techniques such as FMEA (failure modes and effects analysis).

3 **Changes in the marketplace**. These are risks that top management have to consider when preparing their short-term and long-term business plans. There should be a process covering this in the company but, because of its commercial sensitivity, the information will probably not be available outside the board of directors. The output from this process (possibly titled 'Business Planning') will, however, be available to all staff in the form of quality objectives and targets.

4 **Accidents at the workplace**. Safety in the office and on site is described in the Health and Safety at Work Act which led to the publication of numerous regulations that have implications for those working in the construction industry. Typical examples are:

    – The Management of Health and Safety at Work Regulations (MHSWR).
    – The Control of Substances Hazardous to Health (COSHH).
    – Manual Handling Operations Regulations.
    – Construction (Design and Management) Regulations.

    The requirements of the above regulations should be reflected within the QMS, including the measures to be taken to identify identify hazards and their associated risks to health and safety, along with techniques to be used to analyse, eliminate or reduce them – for example, design risk assessments, COSHH assessments, environmental assessments, safety audits and so on.

5   **Technical risks of things going wrong as a result of faults with the design, faults in materials and faults in workmanship**. Preventive measures should, again, be part of the QMS. Research and development design reviews, design risk assessments, design verification and validation, product testing and commissioning are all means of helping prevent failure.

6   **Risks to the business resulting from competition, loss of customers, lawsuits, key staff leaving and failure of the IT systems**. These are all issues for top management. Like those detailed under item 2, these are business risks that must be planned for.

You can't possibly hope to eliminate all risks. But, if you review your business processes, you should be able to identify many of them.

Look at all these risks, the threats they pose, the likelihood of them occurring, and the consequences to the business if they happen, and rank them in importance. Depending on the probability of each one occurring you need to put in the appropriate controls. Where possible, build the controls into your procedures and other QMS documentation.

The family of quality standards

We have covered just a few of the clauses from ISO 9001:2000 with some guidance on their interpretation. Let us now look at other guidance documents that form the suite of the ISO 9000 family of standards.

ISO 9000:2000
Systems – fundamentals and vocabulary

ISO 9000:2000 describes the fundamentals of quality management systems and specifies the terminology for such systems.

The standard provides useful guidance on the following:

- the rationale for quality management
- the QMS approach
- the process approach
- quality policy and quality objectives
- the role of top management within the QMS
- the value of documentation and the types of documentation used in a QMS
- how to evaluate QMSs
- QMSs and other management system focuses
- the relationship between QMS and excellence models.

ISO 9004:2000
Quality Management Systems – guidelines for performance improvements

ISO 9004:2000 provides guidelines that consider both the effectiveness and efficiency of the QMS. The aim of this standard is to improve both the performance of the organization and the satisfaction of customers and other interested parties. We recommend that you read this guideline standard as it contains much more information than ISO 9001:2000.

ISO 9004:2000 takes the ISO 9001:2000 requirements and explains what is needed for an organization to improve itself. It is a valuable tool for any quality manager who is setting out to bring the company's ISO 9001:1994-based QMS to the current standard ISO 9001:2000 *and beyond*.

A 'gap analysis' – that is, an 'as is' to 'as ought' comparison – can be carried out based on the information contained in this standard.

Chapter **3**

Establishing a QMS

Setting the scene

You are now ready to move forward to the business of setting up a QMS that is 'right for you' and structured to satisfy the criteria we listed in the Preface. The best way of accomplishing this is to follow a sequence of logical steps, each building upon the one previous to it. We have used this approach for many years and have found it to be a very successful way of achieving a cost-effective 'right first time' result.

For the purposes of describing how to set up a QMS we are going to use a hypothetical construction design organization which offers the following services to its clients:

- design project management involving:
  - civil design
  - structural design.
- planning supervisor services if required.

Please note that it is the methodology, not the imaginary organization, that we wish to emphasize. The process described can be successfully followed regardless of the nature of your organization.

Case Study: A Hypothetical Situation

The organization uses external support for services such as mechanical and electrical design work when necessary. It has a well-maintained technical library as well as modern computer equipment which is used for functions such as stress calculations, Computer-aided Design (CAD), word-processing and so on. The organization does not have site contracting capabilities, but advises its clients concerning suitable appointees if asked to do so. Although the organization does have a manual of design practice and some general administration procedures, these do not reflect the expectations of any recognized quality management standard.

The organization is increasingly being asked to demonstrate a formal quality management capability when bidding for work and knows that it has lost bid opportunities because of its inability to meet this request. It is also hoping to enter into a number of partnership arrangements, but again is finding the lack of a QMS a major barrier to being able to do so.

Consequently it has decided to set up a formal QMS in order to overcome these problems, become more competitive and cost-effective, and, hopefully, increase its market share. ISO 9001:2000 will be used as the basis.

Lack of a QMS can exclude you from bidding for work.

A senior member of staff who has had extensive quality management experience elsewhere has been identified. This person who has witnessed firsthand the benefits which can be gained from the effective use of a well-structured QMS, has willingly accepted the responsibility of leading this new initiative and will report progress on a monthly basis to the main board of directors.

The board appreciate that time and resources will need to be committed to the task, but are confident that it will be a worthwhile exercise. They also realize that, at times, there will inevitably be a conflict of interests between resources needed (particularly people) to help develop the QMS and working on fee-earning tasks, which are the lifeblood of the business.

Because of this, a target timescale of 15 months has been set for getting a formal QMS in place. The acting quality manager will be allowed to make the task a priority for up to 30 per cent of his time.

He has been asked to prepare an action plan for submission to the board within one month, defining what he considers to be an efficient way of achieving the objective.

Let us now imagine that you are that acting quality manager.

Assessing your position

First of all let us consider what you already know.

You know that any QMS you introduce needs to be accepted by staff at every level within the organization. In other words there will need to be a proper understanding of it, commitment to it and a sense of ownership of it if it is ever going to really work. These things, however, will never be brought about by imposition. This means that drafting the system in isolation and then expecting others to accept and commit to it is a non-starter.

Drafting your QMS on your own and then just expecting people to commit to it is a recipe for disaster.

Achieving the best outcome requires the participation of as many people as possible. You want people to contribute, to feel that they and their inputs are important (as indeed they are) and that, whatever system results, it is *their* system.

You also know that your system is going to be process-based and that at an early stage you will need to identify your key processes and who has the ultimate responsibility for them, so that changes and improvements can be done under proper authority.

Within these key processes will be many sub-processes. These are likely to require documents (such as procedures or instructions) to ensure that they are consistently implemented in ways which are agreed as appropriate at this stage.

You will need to know the output expectancies of your processes in order to allow the monitoring and measurement of their effectiveness; this, in turn, will enable continuing improvement. You have as a reference the ISO 9001:2000 standard.

Finally, because the organization has been reasonably successful for many years, it must obviously be doing many things well and therefore have a considerable number of good practices to build upon. This means that you will not therefore merely change things for change's sake, needlessly sacrificing good, well-tested methods. Instead, you will look critically at what you do and 'how', and then build on your strengths whilst being honest enough to accept your weaknesses and do something about them.

The initial steps

Your first two steps are as follows:

1 Prepare your draft action plan and gain the approval and commitment of the board.
2 Then (and only then) hold a meeting with all staff, including all members of senior management, thus allowing them to share their commitment to the initiative and where appropriate, participate in the presentation. (This may involve explaining why it has been decided to set up a QMS and your role in the exercise, and also encouraging people's participation in, and support for, the action plan to be described in the next section.)

Involving people means being ready to change your plans in response to their feedback.

You will then go through the action plan qualifying the various steps, allaying any suspicions, inviting everyone's involvement and assuring everyone that they will be kept aware of progress and also given the opportunity to test the new system, insofar that it applies to what they do, before it is ever formally introduced.

Finally, answer any questions raised during this presentation fully and frankly.

The action plan: actions, timing and resources

These are the activities proposed to, and accepted by, the board.

Preliminary actions

a) Prepare the plan and gain board approval
b) Launch the plan through a staff awareness meeting.

Subsequent actions

1 Collect information on current organization structure, responsibilities and interfaces *[This can be done by reference to current organization charts, descriptive texts and direct discussions.]*

2 Identify the key processes of the business, their inter-dependencies, ownerships and deliverables (in measurable terms). Agree these with the board.

3 If necessary, amend information on the organization and people's responsibilities to reflect ownership of key processes.

4 With reference to ISO 9001:2000 expectations and the key processes, identify envisaged sub-processes and their scopes. *[That is, identify activities that suggest the need for a procedure or instruction if you are to achieve a consistency of approach]*.

5 Decide formats for procedures and instructions.

6 Prepare a guideline instruction concerning the key considerations to be given when drafting procedures and instructions.

7 Prepare 'information-gathering sheets' for future use by the people chosen to be involved in procedure drafting.

8 Hold a staff meeting to give a progress update and encourage participation in the next phase of the exercise – namely, drafting procedures. *[In conjunction with senior management identify who is to be involved in drafting procedures, selecting them on the basis of their ability, not simply on their availability.]*

9 Allocate to each person an area which is compatible with their knowledge and experience. Advise each of them on the scope of their intended procedure, how to use the 'information-gathering sheets' and how to actually gather the necessary information, including a review of any existing documentation. *[Set a timescale for this work.]*

10 Those selected gather relevant information and record it on their information-gathering sheets

11 The acting quality manager undertakes the preparation of those procedures identified as required in ISO 9001:2000 – namely:
   – document control
   – control of records
   – corrective action
   – preventive action
   – control of non-confirming product
   – internal audits

   plus activities such as:
   – control of the quality manual
   – preparation of procedures/instructions
   – management reviews.

12 Following the completion of action 10, conduct a one-day meeting of the procedure writers. Explain the techniques for writing procedures and the format to be used. Hand out and explain the guideline instruction referred to in action 6. Ask the writers to convert their gathered information into draft procedures. Display the drafts and invite peer review from other writers. Amend the drafts as necessary.

13 Allocate additional procedure subjects for the procedure writers to develop within a suitable timescale.

14 Gather together a review team of people who know the processes involved and invite them to review the draft procedures, support instructions and standardized forms. Amend the procedures in response to the reviews. These reviews should take place at regular intervals as drafts become available.

15 Decide and agree with the board the structure and content of a quality manual and draft the necessary text.

16 Hold a progress meeting with the staff. Thank everyone for the support given to date. Explain the structure of the proposed quality manual. Invite constructive feedback from everyone throughout the planned forthcoming trial period of the system. Ask for volunteers who would be interested in undergoing training as auditors.

17 Train selected staff in auditing techniques.

18 Prepare generic audit checklists.

19 Compile a draft manual and issue on a trial basis.

20 During the trial period invite the auditors to carry out some initial audits in order to develop their technique and confidence, and to provide information on the effectiveness of the new system.

21 Collect and review feedback from all sources on a continuing basis and improve the system where necessary.

22 Conduct a final pre-release check of the system and issue it formally under the appropriate controls.

Post-introduction

- Continue auditing.
- Encourage feedback.
- Carry out management reviews.
- Seek continual improvement.
- Consider third-party certification.
- Select a suitable certification body.
- Obtain certification.

Figure 3.1 shows a timescale for completing the action plan activities within the 15-month period.

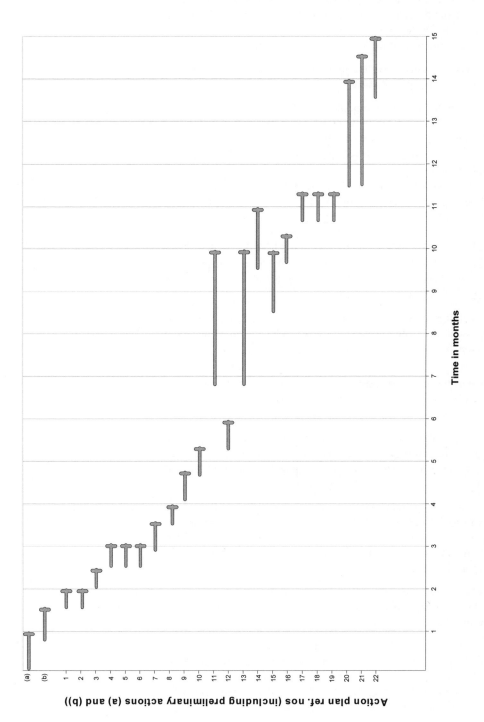

Figure 3.1 *Chart showing target completion dates for action plan activities*

To some people, 15 months may seem to be a short time; to others it may seem long. In our experience it is a reasonable timescale for an organization of the type in question that is starting from scratch, needs between 20 and 30 procedures and is using a pool of six people for procedure writing.

However, in reality the time taken to set up such a system will depend on a number of variables – namely:

- the 'complexity' of the organization's work, not necessarily its size
- management commitment to achievement
- the resources which can be made available for tasks such as procedure writing
- what already exists by way of good systems documentation which may be usable without change or with only minor adaptation.

Building on any good systems documentation you already have is a great way to start.

What is certain, however, is that, if you adopt the methodology and suggested document formats described in the action plan and the following related text you will save a great deal of time in setting up a QMS that is 'right for you'.

We will now move on through the action plan, look at *some* of the key activities and provide a little relevant guidance and justification.

Recording your current set up (action plan – action no. 1)

You need to begin somewhere, and a sensible first step is to establish and record how the organization is currently structured to do what it does – in other words, who is responsible to whom and for what.

How are your people used to undertake what may be a very variable range of project activities? All too often within organizations, people assume that others carry out certain tasks when in reality they may not or, even if they do, it may not really be within their responsibility remit.

You need to be sure that, if you need guidance or a decision, you know who is the right person to turn to, not merely the one having the friendliest ear.

If you are going to define responsibilities on a process basis as opposed to, say, a departmental basis, then some changes may be needed. Good sources for gathering this initial information are any existing organization charts, the human resources department, plus direct discussions with managers and colleagues.

Figure 3.2 and the following text describe the situation in our hypothetical organization.

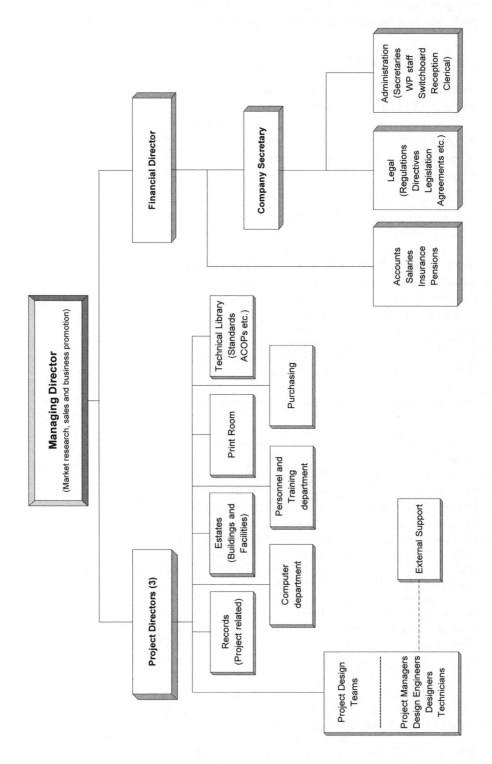

Figure 3.2 *Current organization structure*

Case Study:
Organization Structure and Responsibilities

The current organization and responsibility structure is led by five directors, one of whom acts as managing director, another as financial director and the remaining three as project directors.

The directors hold monthly board meetings at which they review business performance, finances, resource needs, new purchaser requirements and so on. They prepare periodic business plans and monitor ongoing performance against the same. According to the decisions arising from these meetings, they advise and direct the various functional heads accordingly.

Each Director has specific responsibilities as follows:

The *managing director*, in addition to giving overall direction and coordination to business matters, is directly responsible for market research, sales and business promotion strategies.

The *financial director* is responsible for liaison with the bank, preparing budgets, authorized audited statements of accounts, salaries, insurances, wages and so on. In addition, he has overall responsibility for the legal function, managed by the company secretary, which deals with such matters as directives, legislation, regulations, conditions of contract and so on. He is also responsible for the administration department which provides secretarial staff, general word-processing facilities, the switchboard, reception personnel and so on.

The three *project directors* assume responsibilities for the overall management of individual design projects including negotiation of initial briefs, contract reviews, design team formulation and guidance, project planning, design implementation, verification, reviews and recording, continuing client liaison and ultimate work handover to agreed standards and programmes and for client satisfaction.

Design teams comprise a project manager, senior designers, designers and technicians, selected from an available pool of staff on a project-by-project basis. When necessary, additional resources are obtained through the selective contracting out of design work or engaging temporary contract staff to supplement the core teams.

The support functions are each headed by a manager or specified person, and those involved carry out their tasks in accordance with their individual job specifications under the guidance and/or instruction of their immediate line superior.

In our hypothetical organization, then, it is clear that, although people work to the best of their training and ability, there is a lack of the formal specific responsibility guidance to enhance best practice and ensure consistency of approach that a QMS will hopefully bring about.

Identifying your key processes, interfaces and outputs (action plan – action no. 2)

To run a successful business you need to know the following:

- what your markets and customers want *now*
- what is likely to change in the foreseeable future regarding the above (for example, due to market trends, new regulations, competitive influences and the like)
- what you need to do to meet the changing situation (in terms of resources and so on)
- how you can best promote your current and improved capabilities
- what returns you can confidently predict (maximum, minimum)
- what resources will be required to manage the anticipated forward workload
- how you will best achieve the desired results
- how you will monitor the effectiveness of your performance and achieve continuing improvement (techniques).

On the basis of these fundamentals a limited number of key processes emerge for our hypothetical organization. Figure 3.3, along with the following text, describes these as well as their main interfaces and outputs.

The main *outputs* from each of the key processes shown in Figure 3.3 are as follows:

1 *information and/or reports* on matters which are seen as affecting the present and future prospects of the business, and decisions/options for addressing the same
2 *results of overall evaluations* of the above (along with other considerations, such as outputs from management reviews) together with any revised policy/strategy to redefine business capabilities and give direction to sales and marketing policies
3 *forward indications* of business prospects, timings, resource needs and so on
4 *inputs to project design* in terms of correct and timely support needed (such as adequately trained, qualified and experienced personnel), suitably selected external support, appropriate specialist support services (such as IT) and facilities (including buildings)
5 *design outputs* which fully meet customer/client expectations

6 *feedback to Strategic Planning* concerning improvements/ considerations arising from such sources as:
  - clients (on project performances)
  - internal audit findings
  - 'sub-process' performance indicators.
7 *feedback* identifying scopes for the continuing improvement of the QMS
8 *continuing improved and updated information* concerning the QMS and its application on Project Design activities.

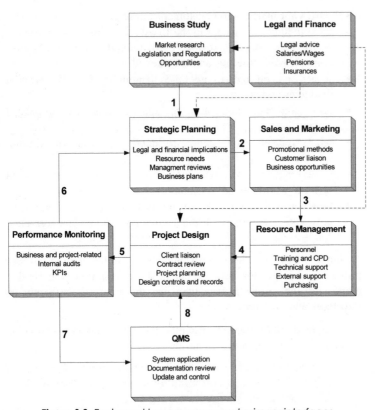

Figure 3.3 *Envisaged key processes and primary interfaces*

Obviously the interfaces shown in Figure 3.3 do not show the whole picture, but they do hopefully illustrate the process approach.

We have given 'Legal & Financial' a separate identity with dotted-line relationships to several of the key processes. This has been done because this function is the provider of specialist, and what may be considered sensitive, information that is not for review by an external audit of the QMS. Examples are information on salaries, costs, fees and profit. This function also gives legal or financial advice on the implications of new laws, directives and regulations to both the Business Study and Strategic Planning processes as well as liaising with Resource Management concerning terms and conditions relating to personnel appointments and for external support services. A similar liaison is maintained with Project Design, advising as necessary on such matters as special conditions of contract.

Adjusting your organization and information about responsibilities (action plan – action no. 3)

Your aim at this stage is to re-express your organization in line with the key processes you have identified. Because you are now introducing a formal QMS there will obviously be some new responsibilities (for example, someone with the duty of overseeing and maintaining the QMS itself) and new functions (for example, internal auditing).

There will also need to be clear process ownerships, performance objectives and mechanisms for continuing improvement. However, this does not mean that you should needlessly dismantle existing functional responsibilities – such as those, say, of the training manager or head of computer services – but that you should recognize that the training and computer functions are but integral parts of a larger process and that unless the process as a whole is successful, then business performance may, or will, be jeopardized.

A number of our key processes such as Business Study, Strategic Planning and Project Design will involve all or several director-level staff in their implementation. Whether or not this is the case, there should be one senior person who has the clear responsibility in respect of *each* key process for:

Regular communication with everyone involved is essential.

- establishing (in agreement with others) the output objectives of the process in measurable terms[*]
- ensuring that those involved in the process are aware of its objectives, aim to meet them and, if designated, gather relevant performance information/data

---

[*] The key processes flow diagram (Figure 3.3) shows that the output from each provides input to the next. If you can then regard your receiver process as an internal customer and determine what that customer needs/expects, you will have a good customer-related guide to output objectives.

Obviously, if part of your output interfaces directly with an external client, then output objectives relating to client satisfaction would apply – for example, keeping to the programme and budget, good communications, cooperation, lack of complaints and so on.

- ensuring that such information/data is made available for collation, review and subsequent consideration at management reviews
- acting as the authorizing authority for the original issues of, or amendments to, process-related procedures/instructions, which relate to the various sub-functions/processes within their particular key process.

This approach ensures *visible* top management commitment. Figure 3.4 (p. 43) illustrates a possible revised organization structure which allocates specific responsibilities for the key processes in a logical way, without any essential alteration to the function groups, whilst accommodating the expectations of the new QMS. The only real change is the transferral of the administration resources from under the company secretary to the Resource Management process.

Thus, in our hypothetical organization our new organizational structure and responsibilities text would read as follows:

Case Study:
Revised Organizational Structure and
Responsibilities

The current organization structure is led by a team of five directors – namely, the managing director, financial director and three project directors, each having the following responsibilities.

Managing Director

The managing director provides overall direction and coordination on business matters. He chairs monthly director meetings and management review meetings at which market opportunities, financial, policy, strategy and resource matters are discussed, and business plans are established and reviewed. In addition to these broad duties, the managing director holds direct responsibility for market research, and marketing, sales and business promotion strategies.

Financial Director

The financial director is responsible to the managing director for all financial matters including, but not limited to, liaison with the company's bankers, arranging financial facilities, preparing annual audited accounts, salaries, insurances, pensions and so on. He is supported by a small team of suitably qualified staff. In addition, he has overall responsibility for the legal section, managed by the Company Secretary, which provides legal advice on such matters as new directives, legislation, regulations and conditions of agreement/ contracts.

Project Director (Resources)

In addition to participating in the monthly director meetings and periodic management review meetings, the project director (Resources) is responsible for the management of specific design projects, including all activities from negotiation of initial briefs, formulation and guidance of dedicated design teams, project design planning, implementation, verification and recording, continuing client liaison and handover of all designs and associated information in accordance with agreed requirements and for ultimate client satisfaction.

In addition, he is responsible to the managing director for the effective management and coordination through the respective functional heads of the following resource functions:

- computer services
- administration services
- personnel and training
- purchasing
- external resource selection
- estates.

Project Director (Design Services)

In addition to participating in the monthly director meetings and periodic management review meetings, the project director (Design Services) is responsible for the management of specific design projects and all associated design activities as described above under project director (Resources).

In addition, the project director (Design Services) is responsible to the managing director for the effective management and coordination through the various function heads of the following design-related functions:

- technical library
- print room
- project records.

Project Director (Quality Management)

In addition to participating in the monthly director meetings and periodic management review meetings, the project director (Quality Management) is responsible for specific design projects and all associated activities as described above under project director (Resources). In addition, he is responsible to the managing director for ensuring through a designated quality manager:

- the establishment and upkeep of the quality management system[*]
- the planning and effective implementation of internal audit programmes
- the provision of guidance to, and training of, staff concerning quality management matters
- liaison with external parties in relation to quality management matters
- the provision of factual inputs to management review meetings with particular emphasis on:
  - internal performance
  - customer/client satisfaction
  - continuing improvement opportunities

plus additional functional responsibilities for:

  - overall health and safety matters
  - control and calibration of measuring and inspection equipment
  - the acceptance of all QMS procedures and instructions.

As can be seen from the text above, all directors have the authority, with respect to the key processes under their control, to exercise their responsibilities for establishing output objectives, ensuring and monitoring people awareness, and for the continuing improvement of their key and integral sub-processes.

Beyond the top-level responsibilities further clarification concerning other responsible staff should follow, taking the sub-sections of each key processes in turn. For example, the manager (Computer Services) is responsible to the project director (Resources) for ... The personnel and training officer is responsible to the project director (Resources) for ... concluding with the duties and responsibility relationships of those working within the project design teams.

You may feel that defining responsibilities to this degree seems like overkill and unnecessary. This is not so. Responsibility is one of the key aspects of any good QMS. It manifests itself basically at three levels.

The *first and highest level*, will almost certainly be within the organization's policy statement which will normally be a very early inclusion within the organization's quality manual. This will make it clear that a QMS is a vehicle to help fulfil the organization's policy and objectives and that it is the responsibility of all concerned to adhere to its principles and requirements insofar that it relates to their duties.

Defining who is responsible for what, at all levels, is key to a successful QMS.

---

[*] For further information regarding the role and responsibilities of the person directly responsible for managing the QMS, see Chapter 4.

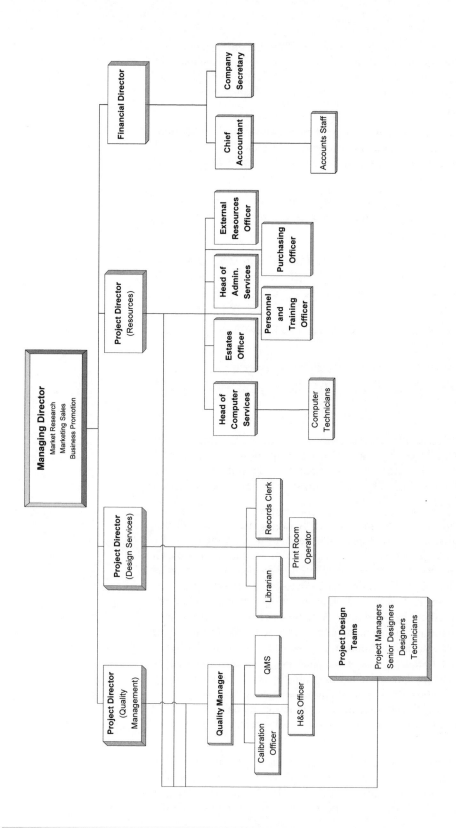

Figure 3.4 *Revised organization chart based on key processes*

The *second level* is to be found within the organization and responsibility charts and supporting descriptive texts, which should make it clear who is responsible to whom and for what. This cuts out ambiguities and disputes as well as providing visible (and auditable) accountability.

There is a very famous statement by the late American admiral, Hyman H. Rickover concerning responsibility, the last sentence of which sums up nicely the significance of this topic. In essence it says:

> *Unless you can point your finger at the person responsible when something goes wrong then you have never had anyone anyone really responsible.*

This visibility is brought even closer to home with a *third level* of documents – namely, procedures which we will be discussing shortly and which define 'what' is to be done, 'how', 'when' (sequence) and by whom.

With a good QMS, responsibility cannot be avoided.

Sub-processes: identification of potential procedures/instructions (action plan – action no. 4)

Your objective at this stage is to try to identify those activities for which you need some formal guidance to help ensure that, whenever the activities in question are carried out, they are implemented in a way which is considered by the organization as best practice (at that moment in time).

There are two main sources of guidance to help you with this task. The first is the ISO 9001:2000 standard itself, which actually stipulates a requirement for six specific procedures, plus much guidance as to the degree of control expected for numerous activities. The second is your own knowledge of the sub-processes. Many of these, such as design changes, design reviews and so on, may be carried out by several different members of the design staff. So, if you expect a consistent approach, then some form of guidance document is indicated. Although the ISO 9001:2000 standard only refers to six specific procedures, most organizations, particularly those who already have established quality systems originally set up against ISO 9001:1994, will already have in place many more procedures than the six indicated in the latest standard. Remember what matters is what is right for the effective management of *your* business.

For an organization such as our hypothetical construction design company, the following are some typical (but not necessarily definitive) procedures which would be helpful. The list, which is offered purely as food for thought, gives first the subject title, followed by those things which the procedure would normally address. Where the title is followed by the letter (c), this indicates that the particular procedure would equally apply to a contractor-type organization.

Beginning with the six procedures listed in the ISO 9001:2000 standard we have:

- **Internal auditing (c)**

  Such a procedure would address:
    - Long-term audit planning
    - Planning individual audits
    - Conducting audits
    - Reporting audit findings
    - Corrective/preventive action initiation
    - Audit reports
    - Action follow-up
    - Audit close-out
    - Records.

- **Corrective action (c)**

  Typical coverage:
    - The receipt recording, development, acknowledgement of problem/non-conforming situation information
    - Problem review and review responsibilities
    - Review considerations
    - Action decisions, authorizations, implementation and recording
    - Collation and ongoing review of problem situations in aim of recurrence prevention.

- **Control of records (c)**

  Typical coverage:
    - Records identification (that is, which records required)
    - Compilation responsibilities
    - Compilation and storage (including environment)
    - Accessibility and traceability
    - Access controls (for example, limitations)
    - Retention periods
    - Reviews and disposals/archiving including responsibilities for same.

- **Control of documents (c)**

  The way in which individual documents are controlled will usually be defined within the specific procedures in which they are referenced. However, an overall procedure, addressing the following principles, is recommended.

  Typical coverage:
    - Receipt, identification, distributions recording of external documents

- Identification, pre-release checks and authorizations of internally produced documents
- Document traceabilities
- Change controls
- Identifications of obsolete documents
- Inclusions of document status (for example, 'for tender purposes only').

- **Control of non-conforming products (c)**
  This procedure may overlap to a degree with other procedures such as auditing, which may identify such problems, and corrective action, which gives an approach for dealing with such situations.

  Typical coverage:
  - Receipt and recording of non-conformance details
  - Situation review and action decisions (aiming at root cause identification and preventive measures)
  - Issuing decision instructions
  - Records and post-action review.

- **Preventive action (c)**
  Within the construction industry there will already be many activities in place which fall under this category. Examples are risk assessments, which aim to identify potential risk situations so that they can be pre-empted, and internal audits, which identify as 'observations' things which, if not attended to, could lead to problems later. For architects, the RIBA *Job Book* provides guidance concerning risk avoidance, plus the entire thrust of the QMS is aimed at getting things right first time.

  The main thrust of a QMS is to get things right first time.

  Typical coverage:
  - Measures taken to identify *potential* non-conformances and their root causes (refer to other procedures if necessary)
  - Evaluation of need for action
  - Deciding action to be taken
  - Recording actions taken
  - Reviewing effectiveness of actions taken.

  All the above six ISO 9001:2000 procedures would normally be among those drafted by the quality manager (or person acting in that capacity). The following are others which would also normally be drafted by that person.

- **Preparation, authorization and control of procedures and instructions (c)**
  Typical coverage:
  - Procedure initiation
  - Information gathering
  - Preparation and review

- – Authorization and acceptance
- – Issue
- – Amendment and update.

All these aspects are covered in detail, later in this chapter.

- • **Compilation and control of the quality manual (c)**
  Typical coverage:
  - – Compilation and the numbering of manuals
  - – Upkeep of the distribution register
  - – Change controls
  - – Records.

- • **Management reviews (c)**
  Typical coverage:
  - – Frequency and purpose
  - – Chairmanship
  - – Attendees
  - – Scope of subjects addressed
  - – Decision recording/minuting
  - – Action delegations
  - – Action effectiveness review.

- • **Training (c) (in conjunction with the training officer)**
  Typical coverage:
  - – Induction training of new staff (including training in the QMS)
  - – Arrangement of initial training
  - – Training for specific tasks
  - – Awareness training concerning new regulations and legislation
  - – CPD
  - – Performance monitoring and review
  - – Temporary staff
  - – Records.

- • **Meetings (c)**
  This procedures can suffice for numerous types of meeting for which formal minutes are produced.
  Typical coverage:
  - – Notifications of meeting
  - – Meeting conduct
  - – Preparation, authorization and issue of minutes
  - – Action monitoring
  - – Records.

- • **Control of inspection, measuring and test equipment (c)**
  Typical coverage:
  - – Acquisition of new equipment
  - – Equipment identification
  - – Storage and protection
  - – Calibration

- Failed equipment
- Use
- Records.

The following would normally be drafted by a person associated with the process concerned.

- **Preparation and use of preferred supplier list(s) (c)**

  Typical coverage:
    - Requirements for inclusion on the list
    - Evaluation techniques
    - List presentation
    - Information confidentiality
    - Using the list
    - Feedback on performances
    - List updates
    - Client recommended suppliers
    - Records.

- **Preparation of bid invitations (c)**

  Typical coverage:
    - Description of requirements
    - Standards to be met
    - Reference to preferred suppliers list
    - Pre-release information checks
    - Authorization
    - Records of distribution.

- **Bid assessments (c)**

  Typical coverage:
    - Persons involved
    - Timing of assessments
    - Criteria considered
    - Decision recording
    - Bidder (successful and otherwise) notification.

- **Control of technical library (c)**

  Typical coverage:
    - Receipt, identifying, registering and filing information/ data
    - Issue and withdrawal controls
    - Traceability
    - Change controls and information update
    - Recall of information
    - Obsolete/out-of-date information
    - Uncontrolled information (for example, suppliers catalogues and their use).

- **Selection and verification of computer software (c)**

  Typical coverage:
    - Determining parameters of applications

- Specifying requirements
- Evidences of software performance capability (test data or programmes)
- Identification of the information (for example, by version number)
- Pre-use virus checking
- Pre-use performance checks.

- **Risk assessments (c)**

  Typical coverage:
  - When conducted
  - Identification of scope of assessment
  - Techniques used
  - Categorization of implications (for example, seriousness of risk)
  - Determining actions needed (for example, redesign)
  - Initiating actions
  - Post action reassessments
  - Notifications to others (for example, about residual risks)
  - Records.

- **Contract review (c)**

  Typical coverage:
  - Review of brief and resolution of queries
  - Identification of resources
  - Brief acceptance (or otherwise)
  - Re-review of final contract
  - Records.

- **Preparation and verification of drawings and calculations**

  Typical coverage:
  - Drawing methods, checking techniques
  - Correction of errors
  - Final approval, release authorizations
  - Identifications of key calculations
  - Formats and information to be included
  - Verifications
  - Release authorizations
  - Records.

- **Purchasing (c)**

  Typical coverage:
  - Pre-evaluation of purchased product
  - Conditions of purchase and key inclusions
  - Documentation used
  - Pre-release checking and final authorization
  - Records.

- **Virus checking (c)**

  Typical coverage:
  - Software involved

- Check timing
- Checking authority
- Ensuring actions dependent upon findings.

- **Control of design changes**

  Typical coverage:

  - Receipt of design change requests
  - Evaluation considerations
  - Persons involved
  - Standard form(s) used
  - Seeking authority to change (for example, from client)
  - Notification of change decision to others
  - Reviews of necessity for change with regard to implications on other work and preventive measures for the future
  - Records.

- **Design reviews**

  Typical coverage:

  - Purposes
  - Frequencies
  - Convened by
  - Participants
  - Conduct of review (see Meetings procedure)
  - Findings recording
  - Action delegations
  - Action follow-up and further review
  - Records.

- **Preparation and use of project quality plans (c)**

  Typical coverage:

  - When prepared
  - By whom
  - Format(s) used
  - Information contained
  - Authorization
  - How used
  - Change controls
  - Records.

- **Preparation and use of detail quality plans (c)**

  Typical coverage:

  - When used
  - Format
  - Information contained
  - Authorization
  - How used
  - Change controls
  - End of job completion checks
  - Plan sign-off
  - Records.

- **Compilation and control of project file**

  Typical coverage:
    - Purpose
    - How identified
    - How segregated
    - Document filing requirements
    - Document access and removal controls/limitations
    - End of project document completion check
    - File recording and storage.

- **Personnel selections and appointments (c)**

  Typical coverage:
    - Position advertising
    - Initial evaluations
    - Short lists
    - Final selections (for example, interviews)
    - Appointment confirmation and documentation
    - Records.

- **Receipt and control of incoming information (c)**

  Typical coverage:
    - Types of information (for example, letters, faxes, telex)
    - Recording receipts (for example, identifying documents and registering)
    - Forwarding to specific recipients
    - Records/traceability.

- **Continuous improvement of project performance (c)**

  Typical coverage:
    - Identification of KPIs (including client feedback)
    - Information gathering (type and frequency)
    - Information review
    - Action decisions
    - Implementations
    - Post-action monitoring
    - Records.

- **Continuous improvement of business performance (c)**

  Typical coverage:
    - Identifying key performance indicators
    - Measuring actual performance
    - Identifying scopes for improvement
    - Action initiation
    - Post-action monitoring and records.

From our list we can see that, from the 31 procedures identified, 27 of them are as relevant to a contractor organization as they are to our hypothetical construction design organization.

Obviously a contracting organization would also consider additional procedures for activities such as:

- control of site office
- control of site stores
- preparation and use of method statements
- applying for concessions and design changes
- site health and safety
- site meetings
- control of support contractors.

This list would further increase if the contractor concerned was acting as principal contractor under the CDM Regulations 1994 (see Chapter 6).

Procedures and instructions, definitions and formats (action plan – action no. 5)

Definitions

The question is often asked: 'What is the difference between a "Procedure" and an "Instruction"?'

As far as we are concerned, the following applies:

A 'procedure' is a slightly higher-tier document than an 'instruction' and incorporates responsibilities for the carrying out of the activities it contains.

An 'instruction' describes things to be done regardless of who the doer might be. For example: 'Wear protective gloves and goggles when handling glass.'

An instruction will frequently be called up within a procedure – for example, when the procedure may require a specific person to perform an activity or sequence of activities in accordance with an existing instruction.

Procedure formats

Procedures can be laid out in different formats, some of which are more user-friendly than others. The three main types are 'text', 'matrix' and 'minute'. These are described as follows:

- **Text style**

  With this style the responsibilities for carrying out each activity are embodied within the text. If you have a lengthy procedure (for example, four pages long) and several different people involved, it only becomes apparent as to who does what, once you have read the whole procedure, or with a little experience, by trusting to memory.

  This style is not particularly user-friendly, can be time-wasting and (because of distractions while reading or a faulty memory) lead the reader into errors of oversight or omission.

- **Matrix style**

This lends itself particularly well to process-type procedures which have cross-function interface boundaries, albeit coming under a single authority.

By the use of a table of key players plus references, the actual procedural activities can be expressed in the form of a matrix-type layout under the separate headings of: 'Activity', 'Responsibility', 'Controlling Document(s)' and 'Records'.

Figures 3.5 and 3.6 show examples of layouts for the front and continuation pages of a matrix-type procedure. The reader-friendly benefit of having a 'responsibility' column will be obvious.

- **Minute style**

This identifies on its front page, under a specific 'Responsibilities' heading, all persons responsible for carrying out procedural activities, first by job title (for example, 'chief designer') and by abbreviation (for example, CD).

In the procedure proper all responsibilities are taken out of the actual text and put in their abbreviated form in a separate right-hand column, similar to the minutes of a meeting.

This format is, again, very reader-friendly as it enables people to see at a glance where they have a part to play.

Figures 3.5 and 3.7 show typical examples of the front and continuation pages for this type of procedure.

Make sure you indicate clearly who is responsible for different parts of each process.

Process/Function		Page 1 of 4			
Procedure Title:	**Procedure No GP10**	**Issue**	1		
Meetings:		**Date**	11/1/04		

1 Introduction
This procedure concerns all meetings for which formal minutes are to be produced, actions delegated, monitored and reported.

2 Scope
This procedure covers:
   a) meeting arrangements
   b) meeting conduct
   c) decision and action recording
   d) preparation, authorization and issue of minutes
   e) action monitoring and recording.

3 Responsibilities
Chairperson   C
Minutes Secretary   MS
Attendees   A

4 Procedure
See continuation pages.

Authorized by:		Date:	
Accepted by:		Date:	

Figure 3.5 *Procedure front page layout suitable for either matrix- or minute-style procedures (including sample text)*

Shortly we will use a matrix-style format for the purpose of information gathering. For the procedures proper, however, we recommend that the minute-style be used. We do not advocate the use of a text style because of the disadvantages described.

The pages of procedures will normally consist of a head page and continuation pages.

The Head page

On the head page the following information and headings will normally be included:

- **Title**

  Our procedure concerns a specific task or sequence of activities and should be titled accordingly: for example, 'Control of Design Changes'.

- **Unique Reference**

  In addition to its title each procedure should carry a unique reference, for example, PP6, which means that it was Project Procedure No. 6.

  This reference number, along with its title, besides appearing on the head page, would also be listed in any index of procedures in the quality manual.

- **Page number**

  Many procedures will have several pages. Each page should be clearly numbered with its own page number and the total number in the set: for example, page 3 of 4.

- **Amendment status**

  The contents of procedures will change from time to time. When this happens the procedure will be subject to amendment. It is important that you know that you are working to the correct version, so the procedure's amendment/issue status is an important piece of information.

  Most procedures will also indicate the date of each issue/update.

- **Authorization**

  Procedures are controlled documents and issued under the authority of an appropriate person.

  In the case of our procedures, this will be whoever carries overall responsibility for the key process under which the procedure in question falls.

- **Acceptance**

  This signature will normally be that of the person having overall responsibility for the QMS. It is not related to the working requirements of the procedure, but signifies that the procedure has been correctly presented and authorized (that is, in accordance with any procedure for writing procedures), that it is compatible with other procedures and QMS requirements, and that it is also compatible with the requirements of the benchmark standard ISO 9001:2000.

Note that procedures prepared by the quality manager and relating to his own areas of direct responsibility will carry just the one signature for both authorization and acceptance.

Ignoring the text-style procedure, there will normally be four main headings under which the matrix- and minute-style procedures will be written. These are:

1 **Introduction**
   This will consist of a description of what the procedure is about.

2 **Scope**
   This incorporates a description of the parameters of the procedure, often expressed under appropriate subheadings.
   For example:
   a) information gathering
   b) information review
   c) action minuting and reporting
   d) implementation
   e) follow-up and review
   f) records.

3 **Responsibilities**
   Under this heading are listed all those involved in implementing the procedure, by both positional/functional title and appropriate letter abbreviations.
   For example:

Project Manager	PM
Quality Manager	QM
Librarian	L

4 **Procedure**
   Under this heading, if the matrix approach is being used, it will merely say 'see matrix overpage'.
   However, if the minute style is being used each separate step in the procedure will be described in sequence.

   Each step will be allocated a unique number (for example, 4.1, 4.2, 4.3) and the person responsible for taking the action/step described will be denoted by their abbreviation in a 'responsibilities' column on the right.

Figure 3.5 shows a typical head page layout for either a minute- or matrix-style procedure.

Continuation pages

These will not normally contain as much information in their format as the head page. The following, however, should be evident:

- procedure title
- procedure reference number
- page number
- number of pages within the set
- issue status.

The formats of continuation pages differ significantly depending on the procedure style. Figures 3.6 and 3.7 show how two imaginary identical actions from a procedure would be presented in the matrix and minute styles respectively. Note that both the head and continuation pages carry unique form numbers and would be standard forms.

Instructions

Like procedures, instructions are controlled documents issued on the authority of an appropriate person. They differ, however, in that they will obviously carry the word 'instruction' instead of 'procedure' and will not include discrete responsibilities for the actions described.

Otherwise, information such as title, page number and authorization still remain.

Postscript

As an alternative to the procedure formats we have discussed, some organizations may opt for a flow diagram approach. This is fine, provided that the diagram in question does not merely illustrate a sequence of actions to be taken without making it clear who has the responsibility for them, how they are required to be carried out and details of any records and distributions required.

Documentation on every procedure should balance the need to simplify the process so people can understand it, against the danger of omitting key details.

Whilst a flow diagram can often be the ideal way of conveying information, it is important that you don't opt for pictoral simplicity at the expense of conveying the important information needed to implement our procedure properly. Without this information the effectiveness and efficiency you are aiming for will be jeopardized.

Procedure Title: Meetings:		Procedure No GP10	Issue	1	Page 2 of 4
			Date	11/1/04	
Activity No	Activity Description	Responsibility	Controlling Documents		Record(s) Required
4.1	**(a) Meeting arrangement** Notify attendees, one week prior to date of meeting.	CP	Form N32		Copy of N32
4.2	Attendees unable to attend are to nominate a competent deputy and advise CP accordingly.	A			
4.3	**(b) Meeting conduct** Nominate a meeting secretary to take minutes.	CP			Minutes of meeting
4.4	Conduct meeting in accordance with agenda and ensure all attendees are given an opportunity to participate.	CP			

Figure 3.6 Typical continuation sheet for a matrix-style procedure (with example inclusions)

Process/Function		Page of			
Procedure Title:	Procedure No GP10	Issue	1		
Meetings:		Date	11/1 /04		
		Responsibility			

	Responsibility
(a) **Meeting arrangement**	
4.1 Attendees are notified of pending meeting by issue of a Form N32 not less than one week prior to date of meeting (copy to records).	CP
4.2 Any attendee unable to attend arranges for a competent deputy to attend, who has the authority to act fully on his/her behalf and advises the CP accordingly.	A
(b) **Meeting conduct**	
4.3 A person is nominated to take minutes (recorded in minutes).	CP
4.4 The meeting is conducted in accordance with the agenda, with all attendees being given a full opportunity to contribute.	CP

Figure 3.7 *Typical continuation page for a minute-style procedure (reproducing information shown in Figure 3.6)*

Procedure writing: spreading the load (action plan – action nos 7 and 9)

You have now reached a very important stage in the development of your system. You have identified some 30 sub-procedures for which you feel it could be helpful to have a procedure, six of which are specific requirements of ISO 9001:2000. You have also identified the scopes that each procedure will, at a minimum, need to cover.

The next step is to spread the task of drafting procedures among a number of suitable people, each of whom is knowledgeable about the sub-process/es) for which he or she is going to draft their procedure(s).

There are several reasons for spreading the load:

- It speeds up the system development process. For example, if you are faced with 24 procedures to draft, it is obviously going to be much quicker to let eight people draft three each, rather than have one person try to write them all.
- By involving people who have a first-hand understanding of the process(es) in question improves the prospects of a successful outcome.

- It gives a greater number of people an understanding of the importance of procedures and the depth of thought that goes into preparing them.
- A wider direct involvement will generate a greater sense of ownership for, and commitment to, the working of 'their' procedure(s).

At this point it should be stressed that when you set up a QMS you have a unique opportunity to make a real impact on the future of your organization. Seldom, if ever, in the lifetime of most organizations does the opportunity arise, to take a deep breath (figuratively speaking), look critically at what you do and ask yourself 'Why?' (that is, 'Are the things we do essential, value-adding, and so on?) and then eliminate what is really not necessary. And, following this, to go further, asking the question: 'Are we doing these essential things in the best possible way in light of current technologies?'

Take time deciding how to word procedures; they will be used for months, and possibly years, to come.

In other words you have the chance to ask those questions mentioned earlier in this book, namely: 'Are we effective?' (doing the right things); 'Are we efficient?' (doing things right). This opportunity must not be missed. Remember when you write a procedure you may be determining the way people are going to do things for months, or even years, to come. You cannot afford to get it wrong.

The first thing you must therefore do with your procedure writers is emphasize to them the importance of the task which they are undertaking. Then allocate to each writer the scope and subject of a first procedure and ask them to gather appropriate information, including any relevant existing procedure(s), instruction(s) or standard forms.

As an aid, issue each writer with a number of blank 'question and answer' sheets on which they can record their information. Figure 3.8 shows the beginning of a typical question and answer form covering the process of design review.

When collecting the information, the information-gatherers should follow a logical trail through the subject process, beginning with the inputs that start the process off and continuing until an end-point is reached. Information-gatherers need to be able to 'think on their feet' remembering Kipling's six stalwart serving men: 'Why', 'Where', 'When', 'What', 'How' and 'Who'.

Remember that, at this stage, you are not asking for them to draft procedures, but merely to gather pertinent information.

The questioning should continue until the scope of the process (as described in the previous section) has been exhausted. Obviously the best person to question first will be a project manager.

Preparation and review of the initial procedures (action plan – action no. 12)

Once the information has been gathered it must be converted into procedures. For this we recommend that you set aside a full day. Gather together all your writers in a suitable room, equipped with an overhead projector. Explain what is to happen, introduce them to the style in which the procedures are to be drafted (say, minute style) and give the guideline information set out in Figure 3.9 in the form of a handout.

Allow two to three hours for preparing the drafts.

Next, ask each writer in turn to display their procedure on the overhead projector, and explain it to the group. The other writers should offer constructive criticism, making points that they feel would improve the procedure, by clarifying or simplifying it, for example.

Encourage discussion of the points raised and ensure they are noted down if accepted as valid. The writer concerned should then amend their procedure accordingly.

Once all procedures have been presented and reviewed, you should have:

- a number of drafted and edited procedures.
- a far better understanding of procedure writing amongst the writers.
- increased confidence on the part of the writers, enabling them to gather the information and draft any additional procedures assigned to them.

If you follow all the steps described above, the procedure drafting process will be off to a flying start.

	Subject	Design Reviews		Contact	Date	Page __ of __
		Activity		-------	-------	
				Responsibility	Document(s)	Record(s)
Q	What are design reviews?					
A	They are stage reviews of technical aspects of the project design programme					
Q	Who attends?					
A	Members of the design team plus any others on the invitation of the project manager					
Q	Who arranges them?					
A	The PM			PM		
Q	How are people notified?					
A	By a memo issued by the PM			PM	Memo of notification	Copy memo

Figure 3.8 *Example of a typical question and answer form with some initial QA information*

Useful guidelines to follow when writing procedures.

- Write positively rather than negatively. For example, write 'This is done ...', 'He does that ...', avoiding conditional words like 'should', or 'may'. Keep the tense consistent.
- Always clearly define who is responsible for carrying out activities.
- Use separate paragraphs for each specific action or requirement and number the paragraphs clearly.
- Reread what you have written several times, asking yourself 'Is it results-oriented?' and 'Is it effective?'. In other words, does it describe those things which really need to be done to ensure the desired result?
- Ask yourself 'Is it efficient?' Have you included the right steps in your procedure but failed to use an appropriate structure or best order for them? Is their way of doing things the best possible at that moment in time?
- Use simple words. Long or complex words might look impressive but, if they confuse, they are counterproductive.
- Keep the text relevant: that is, express only what needs to be done by those directly concerned. Do not waste words by including activities that are the responsibility of others and beyond the control of those for whom the procedure is intended.
- Do not write a procedure at all if something more simple, such as a basic instruction, or a standard form will do.

Keep it simple – do you always need a procedure? Perhaps a simple instruction will do.

Figure 3.9 *Sample handout giving procedure-writing guidelines*

Procedures normally drafted by the quality manager (action plan – action no. 11)

Procedures drafted by the quality manager are of a general nature and an indication as to which procedures they are is indicated in the section 'sub-processes'. However, for convenience here is a suggested list:

- Control of the technical library
- Internal auditing
- Corrective action
- Control of records
- Control of documents
- Control of non-conforming products
- Preventive action
- Preparation authorization and control of procedures and instructions
- Compilation and control of the quality manual
- Management reviews
- Training (in conjunction with the training officer)
- Meetings
- Control of inspection, measuring and test equipment.

Procedure review: the recommended approach (action plan – action no. 14)

In many organizations, as procedures are drafted they are copied and circulated to interested parties for comment. However, we do not recommend this method as it inevitably leads to serious delays while comments are raised, amendments made and so on.

A far better approach is to establish small review groups of knowledgeable people who can get together at regular intervals, to look at draft procedures which relate to their particular process area and make collective decisions about any amendments.

The quality manual: recommended structure and contents (action plan – action no. 15)

ISO 9001:2000 requires an organization to have a quality manual. What should this manual contain and how should its information be presented?

Think for a moment about the prime purposes of such a manual:

1   It is a collective statement of your organization's policy, objectives, responsibilities, processes, working procedures and supporting documents, issued for the benefit of everyone within the organization.

    Its aim is to impart clear understanding about the organization's mission, its management strategies, and to harmonize everyone's efforts by providing guidance on the preferred ways of doing things.

A well-written quality manual can help you win new business.

2   It can be used to provide visible evidence of your capability to others. How this can be done to help win business when bidding for project work will be touched on in Chapter 9 of this book.

You should also remember that the manual is a statement of how your organization does things. Much of the information in it, such as the actual working procedures, you may regard as confidential and you may not wish to disclose them to competitors.

What you really need, therefore, is a manual which enables you to meet the purposes described above, without disclosing those processes which you regard as confidential. We recommend that you use a four-part manual structured similarly to that described in Figure 3.10.

Part 1	• Contents index
	• Amendment history record
	• Definitions and abbreviations
	• List of illustrations
	• Confidentiality statement
	• Profile of the organization
	• Policy statement
	• Key processes
	• Organization and responsibilities
	• Compatibility between the QMS and the ISO 9001:2000 standard
Part 2	• Procedures
	(a) Project-related
	(b) General
Part 3	• Instructions
	(a) Project-related
	(b) General
Part 4	• Standard forms
	(a) Project-related
	(b) General

Figure 3.10 *Suggested format for a quality manual*

Consider your Manual as having four parts.

Part 1 will be a 'General' section and will include:

- manual title and unique copy number (to enable traceability to holders and assist update controls)
- manual contents index
- amendment 'History Record'
- glossary of definitions and abbreviations
- list of figures/appendices
- confidentiality statement
- organization profile (that is, history, type of activities and so on)
- policy statement, including at minimum:
  - recognition of customer and stakeholder needs
  - objectives of meeting them
  - purpose of the QMS and of people's commitment to it
  - commitment to continual improvement).
- key processes – interfaces and outputs (similar to those shown earlier under 'Identifying your Key Processes, Interfaces and Outputs')
- information on organization and responsibilities (similar to the earlier section, 'Adjusting your Organization and Information about Responsibilities')
- statement of compatibility between the QMS and the ISO standard.

Part 2 will include the actual procedures which, within an organization such as our hypothetical construction design company, would probably be grouped under 'Project Specific' and 'General'.

Part 3 will incorporate any 'Instructions' referred to in the various procedures.

Part 4 will incorporate copies of the various standard forms referenced in either the 'Procedure' or 'Instructions'.

One of the advantages of the four-part manual structure is that by showing potential clients only specific sections of the manual – for example, Part 1 plus the index of procedures – you can demonstrate your quality management capability without divulging commercially sensitive information such as actual procedures.

Training internal auditors (action plan – action no. 17)

You need to make sure that your QMS does the job it was designed to do.

Once you have your system in place it is essential to monitor its effectiveness and seek opportunities for the continuing improvement of your business processes, your overall performance and the QMS itself.

Prior to the arrival of ISO 9001:2000 the main thrust of auditing was aimed at checking compliance, mainly against procedural requirements. Although the mechanism of audit planning implementing, reporting and corrective action implementation is essentially unchanged, the subjects of the audits and the checklists used are now much more reflective of factors such as visible management commitment, processes, and the understanding of processes, people participation and continuing improvement.

It is not possible to go through the subject of auditing in detail in a book such as this. For over 20 years we have run auditor training courses which carry some 80 pages of notes. It is not a subject that can be treated lightly.

Those who have already gained third-party certification from an accredited certification body will be well aware that one of the prime interests of such bodies is how well you are monitoring yourself.

Audits can fall into different categories, namely:

- 'system audits', which will test all parts of the QMS over a time period
- 'project audits', which will concentrate on the application of the QMS to specific projects or project stages
- 'process audits', which follow a process trail and have assumed greater prominence since the arrival of ISO 9001:2000.

The big advantage of project and process audits is that they both test functional interfaces.

For those embarking down the QMS route, we suggest you have a number of suitable staff formally trained in auditing techniques.

Trial introduction of the system: feedback and initial audits (action plan – action nos 19 and 20)

Having developed your system and produced your quality manual it is now time to run the system for a trial period. There are several reasons for this:

- You promised at the outset that everyone would be given the opportunity to try to work to the system prior to it being formally introduced.
- Everyone needs the opportunity to identify difficulties, and/or suggest further improvements.
- Newly trained auditors will need to carry out limited scope audits, develop their skills, build up their confidence as auditors and provide a second source of feedback.

It is possible to speed up the process by introducing procedures for trial, following their acceptance by their review panel.

On the bar chart which accompanied the action plan (Figure 3.1), a period of some three to four months was allowed for the trial period.

System amendment and formal issue (action plan – action nos 21 and 22)

As the information is received from your various feedback sources, it will be considered by the relevant review panel along with your acting quality manager. All points will be considered, accepted fully, or in part, or rejected.

In all cases you should thank the person who raised the point for their input, advise them of the decision and, if necessary, give the reason for that decision.

Once the QMS has been amended in accordance with the accepted amendments, you should send uniquely numbered copies of the first edition of the manual to named individuals to be used by them and people in their work areas. The quality manager should hold a record of distribution.

You are now on your way.

Chapter **4**

The Role of the Quality Manager

The role and responsibilities of the quality manager (or person having overall responsibility for the management for the QMS) are described below. However, before we look at what is expected of the quality manager we first need to select a suitable individual to take on the role.

Choosing the quality manager

ISO 9001:2000, clause 5.5.2 makes it the responsibility of top management to appoint a member of management (generally referred to as the quality manager) who, irrespective of other responsibilities, shall have responsibility and authority to carry out duties in relation to maintaining the QMS. These are as follows:

1 Ensure that processes needed for the QMS are established, implemented and maintained.
2 Report to top management on the performance of the QMS and any need for improvement.
3 Ensure that awareness of customer requirements is promoted throughout the organization.

All too often the choosing of an individual to be a quality manager is done without considering whether the person is suitably qualified to take on the role. You would not consider employing an architect or project manager without the necessary qualifications, background experience and training to fulfil the position, so don't rush into appointing a quality manager.

You wouldn't appoint an architect without first checking their credentials. Make sure you take the same care when appointing a quality manager.

The person selected for the position of quality manager should ideally possess the following attributes:

1 **Qualifications and training:**
   – a technical qualification in an engineering or science discipline (degree, HND, HNC or similar)
   – membership of the Institute of Quality Assurance (prefer-ably)
   – safety training (preferably)
   – environmental training (preferably)
   – auditor training
   – computer training.

2 **Experience**
   – a number of years' experience in the industry, including experience of quality management
   – a good knowledge of the working processes and interfaces between all functions in the organization or a similar organization
   – Experience in dealing with people at all organizational levels.

3 **Other attributes**
  - good listening skills
  - presentation/communication skills
  - documentation writing skills
  - a proactive attitude
  - tolerance and fair-mindedness.

In other words, the potential candidate needs to be multi-skilled and very versatile.

Roles and responsibilities

The quality manager has a diverse and important role to play. In a small organization (say, an architectural practice or design consultancy) where everyone is based at a single office the quality manager could carry out all the duties while also managing other roles within the company – for example, those of safety manager, environmental manager, standards manager and records manager. However, with a large construction organization, especially if it is based at several locations or operating on a number of sites, some tasks will need to be delegated.

The following are typical of the duties that a quality manager could be expected to carry out:

A good quality manager will have an effective mix of technical and people skills. Don't pick a technical expert who can't communicate or vice versa.

- *Coordinating the compilation of the QMS:* the quality manager will not be preparing all the documentation comprising the QMS but is responsible for its issue and availability through the organization.
- *Identifying processes:* ensuring that all new business processes are brought into the QMS.
- *Maintaining the QMS:* reviewing all processes at defined frequencies, amending and reissuing documentation.
- *Establishing any internal or external audit schedule:* overseeing the effective conduct and reporting of audits.
- *Preparing or contributing to the preparation of quality programmes and quality plans:* ensuring that these documents are approved prior to implementation and that they are updated as necessary during the work programme.
- *Acting as the focal point for clients and other external organizations seeking information regarding the QMS:* the quality manager is the focal point for any quality-related issues.
- *Contributing to a 'preferred suppliers list':* one part of the selection criteria should be the supplier's QMS. The quality manager should identify the appropriate quality-related questions to be included on supplier assessments.
- *Preparing quality management clauses for insertion in specifications and purchasing documents:* this is to ensure that the supplier clearly understands his obligations under ISO 9001:2000.

- *Running training courses for staff on the QMS especially new starters who must understand its requirements:* this should include training staff on why the organization has a QMS and the nature of its benefits (which will accrue if the QMS forms the basis for continuous improvement).
- *Attending project meetings where the QMS is on the agenda:* the quality manager can contribute by giving advice on how best to use the QMS for managing projects, managing records, making quality submissions to clients and so on.
- *Maintaining the calibration system:* the calibration system is part of the QMS and must be maintained, whether it be office-based or site-based. The quality manager should oversee its operation.
- *Investigating customer complaints:* another important interface that has to be managed. The quality manager should be responsible for the registering of complaints and arranging responses.
- *Coordinating corrective and preventive actions:* the quality manager should be aware of actions that take place and ensure that solutions are customer-focused and lead to improvements in the QMS.
- *Customer feedback:* it is important that any feedback relating to the QMS is coordinated by one individual and then disseminated throughout the company. The quality manager is well placed to manage the collection of customer feedback, which is an important requirement of ISO 9001:2000.
- *Compilation of records:* records have to be managed, both during project/task activities and once they have been archived. The quality manager should be the 'Owner' of this key process.
- *Management reviews:* the quality manager should make inputs to, and participate in, management reviews.

Possible additional responsibilities

Additional responsibilities in a construction and design consultancy could be:

- controlling the standards library, which may consist of hard copies and an electronic database
- taking part in design reviews as appropriate.

Additional responsibilities in a product manufacturer might be:

- controlling an inspection team
- monitoring 'in process' quality
- goods inwards inspection
- releasing the finished product
- approving new products and processes for production use.

Chapter 5

Project Management

Key parties and interfaces

When we hear of a new major project being launched in the UK, why is it that we suspect that whatever budget figures and completion dates are projected, the reality will almost certainly be major delays, cost escalations, excuses and recriminations? Wherever we look, whether it be aerospace projects, defence contracts, or building projects the story always seems to be the same, in some cases with extra time and money being sought almost as soon as work commences. Why do such situations arise? Why do we repeatedly accept them? The truth is that, in many cases, such situations are almost inevitable, simply because the basis on which the project has been launched has not been adequately thought through or is too vaguely defined, with the result that 'in progress' changes become necessary, disrupting both project timescales and cost predictions. Even worse, in some cases, difficulties have resulted in a dilution of original specifications and can compromise results. In Figure 5.1 the simple curve relating to construction projects indicates the implications of having to make corrections in relation to costs on a typical construction project.

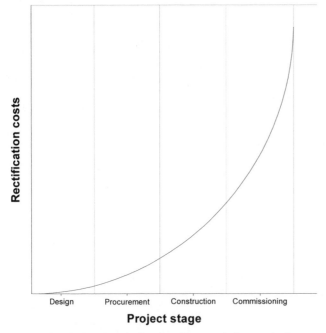

Figure 5.1 *Graph showing the escalating cost of rectifying work with each project stage*

The curve tells us a few rather obvious truths:

- It is far less expensive to consider things properly during the design stage, when changes/corrections have the least 'knock-on' effect.

- Once the project has advanced to the purchase phase, when materials may have been ordered, and the implications of order cancellations, reordering, delayed deliveries and so on become a factor, then the resulting 'knock-on' effects in terms of additional administration costs and extended project timescales become increasingly likely.
- By the time the project has reached the on-site stage, numerous factors such as adverse weather conditions, access problems, dismantling existing structures, delays to the work of others engaged on adjacent activities, reprogramming and enforced waiting times, can enter the picture, with all the obvious implications for project timescales and costs.

All the above is well known. Why is it then, we may ask, that at the beginning of a project there never seems to be enough time to get things right, whilst there always seems to be time at the high end of the cost scale to put things right when they have gone wrong?

At heart, most people want to do a good job, and they take pride in doing so. It is not helpful to good project spirit, however, when people are required to work under pressure to recover project timescales rectifying situations not of their making and which could have been avoided with a little more attention earlier in the project. Although Figure 5.1 may seem to indicate a need for more emphasis at the design stages, it is not merely a question of design.

Seventy per cent of the root causes of the most expensive project disasters come down to basic shortcomings in research, specifications, planning and training.

In the past, surveys have been carried out in an attempt to identify the root causes of expensive failures or disasters. These have shown that more than 70 per cent of all root causes could be traced to things that should have been done, but were not done or at least not done adequately, before anybody started to do anything in the practical sense. In other words, the problems could be traced back to such things as:

- lack of adequate research/test
- poor specifications
- poor planning
- inadequate training.

If any of the above is not done properly, everything that follows is compromised. This means that we should all make a conscious effort to get things right from the very outset on every project.

During our careers both of us have been responsible for the application of quality management on some very large, multi-disciplinary, high-technology projects, which included major construction works with very significant health and safety implications as well as very firm completion dates.

The fact that most of these huge projects were completed on time and within budget was due to many factors, not least to good management, communication and coordination. Another very important factor, however, was that, from start to finish, everything was carried out under the umbrella of a quality management approach which embraced not only all the 'in-house' activities of the parent organization, but also included the pre-assessment, selection and ongoing monitoring of the numerous supporting design consultancies, design and build contractors and other contractors and suppliers throughout the UK. The methods used were really quite straightforward and, as such, applicable to any project, whether large or small. Certainly they provided a visible and sound basis for the control of project activities which, equally importantly, was acceptable to a very strict monitoring and licensing authority.

If a project is to be brought to a successful conclusion, there are a number of basic requirements which need to be met. The following is not a definitive list, but certainly a highly relevant one.

- Those involved need to be chosen on a *known* ability to resource, manage and undertake their assigned responsibilities.
- Those responsibilities must be clearly defined in a formal and definitive manner and any ambiguities/misunderstandings resolved *before* appointments are made.
- Responsibilities, their limitations and interfaces need to be clearly defined.
- Activities need to be planned, coordinated and monitored, with a view to meeting specific defined objectives.
- There need to be *clear* and *understood* communication routes.
- All parties need to work together with a common objective – namely, a successful project outcome.

We will now briefly look at some of the above points (which in reality are no more than the application of common sense and reflected within such documents as ISO 9001:2000 and the 1994 CDM Regulations) in a little more detail.

Selecting according to known abilities

The first point we touched on was that of choosing organizations or people having the known ability to do what is expected of them in every respect. This applies to the full range of appointments likely to be made – for example, architect, design consultant, planning supervisor, principal contractor and other contractors. Depending on the nature of the appointment, it will include such factors as financial stability, technical ability, adequacy of resources, health and safety awareness, quality management capabilities, track record and so on.

In some cases, those who may not be actually making appointments can be tasked with making reliable recommendations to others – for example, architect to client. Such people equally have an obligation to ensure that their recommendations are founded on known information; if they do not, they do their client and themselves a disservice and may jeopardize the project.

If things go wrong because of some basic inadequacy of an appointee, there is little point in looking for a scapegoat and blaming that appointee, when the real culprit was probably yourself for not carrying out a proper evaluation in the first place.

*The only time you can safely award a contract purely on the basis of price is when you **know** that each of the tendering parties **fully satisfies all your other criteria**.*

Some organizations tend to award work purely on a lowest bid basis. This, however, is only really a valid option if you *know* that those you are comparing satisfy all other criteria fully.

If you are making an appointment and, in so doing, are delegating responsibility for the appointee to appoint others (such as support contractors) in turn, then one of the factors that will need to be considered is the appointee's evaluation procedures for choosing such further support services. Failure to do this could lead to a serious dilution of performance quality and project problems. (Internally, of course, with regard to your own personnel it is expected that there will be a 'skills register' or similar, recording the competence of individuals, from which to select the right people for the tasks to be performed.)

Having the right organizations in place within the overall project structure is critically important, as is the provision of an appropriate QMS. Appointing the right organization helps you 'manage by exception'; you have confidence that those involved have in place the management and controls required to: evaluate accurately what is to be done; plan and programme activities; adhere to specified requirements; verify outputs; review against plans; identify and correct adverse situations; and monitor their own performances. With the confidence that these things are happening, the role of overall project management becomes less onerous and allows more opportunity to concentrate on matters such as coordination and overall monitoring, as opposed to 'fire-fighting' on numerous fronts. Chapter 8 deals with choosing support services in detail.

Defining responsibilities and resolving ambiguities and misunderstandings

Our second point relates to all the various parties engaged on a project understanding their exact responsibilities. This was the purpose in the ISO 9001:1994 standard of contract review.

Before any contract is awarded there needs to be a clear understanding between both the appointer and appointee as to exactly what is to be done, what the limitations are, what will constitute acceptable achievement in measurable terms and so on.

If at this stage any party can see scope for simplification or improvement, now is the time to discuss and incorporate it, if appropriate. Any client should welcome constructive suggestions at this stage, and it is likely to strengthen the client–customer relationship.

Defining the limits and interfaces of responsibilities

Our third point concerns individual responsibilities. We have already stressed in Chapter 3 the importance of having clearly defined responsibilities, so that people know where to turn when they seek advice or authority to pursue a particular course of action.

For example, someone on site may have authority to approve minor structural changes, but should these impinge on the actual structural design or might involve health and safety considerations, then the responsibility for making a decision would automatically be referred to the appropriate design authority, who is in a better position to assess the wider implications involved. The history of project disasters is littered with occasions when people, often under pressure and with the best of intentions, made decisions without appreciating their full implications.

Effective decision-making on site means that everyone should know when they can and when they can't make a decision themselves.

Knowing *who* should be involved and ensuring that they are involved is fundamental. Pressures to do otherwise should be resisted. Often, those exerting such pressures will be conspicuous by their absence when things go wrong.

Responsibilities on a project should be clearly defined in documents such as project quality plans. These are dealt with in some detail in Chapter 7.

Planning, coordinating and monitoring responsibilities

Our fourth point refers to 'planning' which basically means thinking through in advance what needs to be done, how, by whom and in what sequence, then identifying the necessary resources and expressing things in a manner which is clear to all and which can be monitored and used as a vehicle for ongoing project control. Again, Chapter 7 addresses these issues.

Setting up clear and understood communication routes

Our fifth point concerns the need to have defined communication routes. It is impractical and counterproductive to have everyone talking to everybody else across project interfaces.

It is important that communication takes place between people who have the appropriate knowledge or level of responsibility, otherwise the inevitable outcome will be chaos, confusion, loss of control or worse.

The communication links between these people should be formally identified and can be included, if necessary, in documents such as project quality plans.

Working with a common objective

Our final point concerns everyone having a common objective. One of the best vehicles for maintaining overall focus is the project team meeting which, if well conducted, can offer the many benefits described in Chapter 7.

Chapter **6**

The CDM Regulations 1994

The impact of the Regulations on the construction industry

An organization can freely choose whether or not it introduces a formal QMS, but there is no such choice concerning compliance with the CDM Regulations if they apply to your construction activities. Whether such activities are notifiable and applicable is described under Regulation 13.

The Regulations require that you place greater emphasis, and give more thought to, identifying potential causes of risks to health and safety. In addition, as far as is reasonably practicable, you must take measures to eliminate or reduce such causes and, if elimination is not fully possible, make others who may be affected aware of any remaining hazards, so that they can take appropriate action(s).

In Chapter 5 we emphasized the importance of paying close attention to front-end activities such as design and planning. The Regulations also recognize this importance by bringing health and safety issues on a compulsory basis into these phases of the construction process, with one of the most visible aspects being the introduction of a new appointment – namely, the planning super-visor – with respect to the project team.[*]

It is also interesting to note how the effectiveness of the Regulations depends on the points we listed in Chapter 5 – namely:

- ensuring that organizations and individuals are selected on the basis of their *known* capabilities and resources
- clearly defined responsibilities with accountability parameters
- good inter-party communications
- proper planning, including giving visibility to health and safety considerations and situations.

In other words, good project and safety management are based on common principles which can readily be integrated into your QMS. This allows for the subsequent monitoring of their effectiveness by techniques such as internal audits. Health and safety matters are too important to be left to the varying (albeit well intended) standards of individuals. There needs to be formality, visibility and under-standing about the approaches you use. Your QMS is the vehicle for providing these things.

We will now look in a little more detail at the roles and duties of the main parties involved on a project which is notifiable, subject to the Regulations, and involves significant design work and several contractors.

---

[*]A planning supervisor and principal contractor are not always necessary. See Regulations 3(5) and 3(6).

The roles of the key parties

The client (or appointed agent acting as the client)

The client has a number of duties to perform. These can be summarized under the following four headings:

1   selecting and appointing others
2   providing project-related information to the planning supervisor
3   ensuring, as far as is reasonably practicable, that the construction phase of any project does not start without an appropriate health and safety plan complying with Regulation 15(4)
4   ensuring the proper maintenance and ready availability of the health and safety file for inspection and the subsequent transfer in total or in part of the information contained in it, as and when necessary.

Selecting and appointing others

A first appointment that the client should make is that of a planning supervisor in accordance with Regulation 6(1)(a). In making this key appointment you need to give every consideration to design and project experience, knowledge of the duties to be performed, resources and also types of resource that will be committed (for example, compatible computer facilities), including time.

The reason this appointment needs to be made at an early stage, is to allow the planning supervisor to carry out several tasks, not least of which are:

• provide notification of the project details to the HSE
• work closely with the design team to develop the information provided by the client and produce a pre-tender health and safety plan.

Many organizations, such as design consultants, now offer planning supervisor services. When making such an appointment however, we recommend that it be done on a 'stand-alone' basis, with its own fee structure, in order to reflect the impartial nature of the role and its direct accountability to the client.

A second appointment is that of the principal contractor, in accordance with Regulation 6(1)(b). Although this appointment does not have to be the main contractor, logically this would be preferable.

Again, you need a full understanding of the main duties of the principal contractor in relation to overview, coordination and the provision of guidance to others in respect of health and safety matters, if you are to consider the experience, resources and time commitment of potential appointees. This is a matter for which advice from the planning supervisor can be useful.

It is the duty of the client to ensure that both of the above appointments remain filled throughout the duration of the project although on large multi-disciplinary projects, actual appointees may change.

Any other appointments made by the client, or subject to their approval, need to be made using similar levels of pre-appointment evaluation for the particular duties to be performed (in relation to the Regulations).

As a client, it is important to know that anyone seeking to make a project appointment or recommending an appointee for your acceptance has adequate evaluation procedures in place.

These matters and others relating to different appointments are dealt with in greater detail in Chapter 8.

Providing project-related information to the planning supervisor

Regulation 11(2) defines the scope and extent of the information required, but we offer a brief summary below.

It is very important that the client provides as much information as possible, as early as possible. Failure to do so could delay the design process or, if speculative design begins anyway, could result in abortive work, wasted time and effort, and increased costs. Some clients who may not be closely associated with actual construction may find it difficult to provide the necessary information. Here the guidance of the planning supervisor should be called upon.

We recommend that client organizations which commission projects on a regular basis establish a list of useful information as it provides for a degree of consistency for any factors that may need to be considered on a project-by-project basis. This list can be continually updated as working experiences reveal new factors that merit consideration on future projects.

There are certain basic pieces of information any planning supervisor needs before he can produce a pre-tender health and safety plan.

Obviously no list will ever be definitive. Unfortunately we live in a real world where we are continually learning from our mistakes and striving to prevent their recurrence. The following is a list of useful information. It is not definitive, but purely indicative.

- Site/premises address, description and history
- Planning information, historical and current
- User/occupier details
- Copies of any reports – for example, surveys, studies and so on

- Details of any relevant communications with the Health and Safety Executive
- Project description
- Project completion, purpose and usage intentions
- Any existing health and safety file or relevant information within it
- Legal or statutory constraints or conditions
- Existing structures
- Adjacent premises, uses and constraints (if any)
- As-built drawings (if any)
- Limitations of access
- Environmental factors (for example, emissions, noise contamination and so on)
- Geographical/geological factors
- Underground workings, water courses, mines and so on
- Utilities (gas, water, electric, telecommunication supply systems)
- Hazardous substances
- Special storage or transport requirements
- Special skills and training needs indicated.

Ensuring any project's construction phase does not start without an appropriate health and safety plan

This is a requirement of Regulation 15(4) but does not mean that no construction whatsoever can begin without a health and safety plan covering all the intended construction work. It is acknowledged that, on large projects, construction is likely to take place in stages over a considerable time period.

What is essential is that before the construction of any particular stage (or structure) commences, the health and safety plan that covers this stage has been prepared and has been accepted by the client.

These plans must be made available for the client to agree at an early stage, otherwise delays to the construction programme will result.

Ensuring the proper maintenance and ready availability of the health and safety file for inspection and the subsequent transfer of information therein as required

It is a requirement of Regulation 14(d) that there be a health and safety file in respect of each structure.

The file should contain 'as-built' drawings and other information as defined or generated as a result of the various Regulations. Guidance to what needs to be contained is described in Regulation 14(d) (i) and (ii) and supporting ACOP (Approved Code of Practice).

The planning supervisor

Unless a project is exempt from the Regulations, it is mandatory to appoint a planning supervisor. This is a key role which involves working with most of the other parties concerned on a project – for example, the HSE, client, designer(s) and principal contractor.

Working with the client

Regulation 7(1) requires that, provided that the planning supervisor determines that the project is notifiable, it is their duty on behalf of the client under Regulation 7(1) to notify the HSE in accordance with Regulations 7(2) to 7(4), providing details as specified in Schedule 1, which are known or can reasonably be ascertained on an F10 form. These particulars to be forwarded to the HSE are as follows:

- date of forwarding
- exact address of construction site
- name and address of the client or clients
- type of project
- name and address of planning supervisor
- declaration signed by, or on behalf of, the planning supervisor, confirming his appointment
- name and address of the principal contractor
- a declaration signed by or on behalf of the principal contractor confirming his appointment
- date planned for the start of the construction phase
- planned duration of the construction phase
- estimated maximum number of people at work on the construction site
- planned number of contractors on the construction site
- name and address of any contractors already chosen.

The planning supervisor's day-to-day duties are as follows:

- Ensure that the pre-tender health and safety plan is prepared.
- Provide an ongoing support, guidance and monitoring service with respect to health and safety matters.
- Advise, if required, on the choice and appointment of others.
- Advise on the adequacy of the construction health and safety plan(s) if requested.
- Ensure that health and safety file(s) are prepared for ultimate handover to the client.
- Report, as required, on health and safety matters.

Working with the designer(s)

- Monitor the adequacy of arrangements for health and safety as defined in the Regulations, including those between different design bodies if necessary.
- Monitor the implementation of the above arrangements.
- Liaise with the designer(s), concerning information needed for inclusion within the pre-tender health and safety plan and the health and safety file and ensure that such inclusions are made.

Working with the principal contractor

- Ensure timely availability of the pre-tender health and safety plan.
- Provide advice, if requested, on the selection and appointment of others.
- If requested by the client, advise on the pre-construction availability and suitability of the construction health and safety plan(s).
- Maintain a close liaison to ensure the timely production of information needed for inclusion in the health and safety file.
- Ensure that a health and safety file is prepared.

The designer

The Regulations define designers as organizations or individuals carrying out design work, including architects, consultants, quantity surveyors, chartered surveyors and technicians, whilst the term 'design' includes drawings, design details, specifications and bills of quantity.

The duties of the designer are defined in Regulation 13 and can be broken down as follows:

Regulation 13(1)

Under Regulation 13(1) the designer must take reasonable steps to ensure that the project client is aware of the duties to which the client is subject by virtue of the Regulations and of any practical guidance issued from time to time by the Commission with respect to the requirements of the same.

This is an important action and we recommend that it be done in writing.

Regulation 13(2)

Regulation 13(2)(a)(i) requires the designer to ensure that any design prepared and intended for the purposes of construction will include design considerations with respect to *avoiding foreseeable risks* to the health and safety of anyone involved in construction and cleaning work on the structure at any time or of any person who may be affected by the work of such a person at work.

Regulation 13(2)(a)(ii) goes on to ask for consideration of the need to *combat at source* risks to health and safety of such persons as described in (i) above.

Regulation 13(2)(a)(iii) asks that *priority* be given to measures which will protect *all* persons who carry out the work described in (i) and (ii) above (or who may be affected by their work) over measures which only protect each person carrying out such work. For example, in the case of a risk of contact with a hazardous substance, a measure that might protect each individual would be to use protective clothing. A preferred measure (if viable) would be one that eliminated the risk entirely – for example, by removing, in advance, the source of the problem or by relocating the work to a safer location.

The obligation on the designer to carry out appropriate risk assessments, consider safer construction options and include, in the design, measures to aid safe construction is obvious. They will need to work closely with the planning supervisor who will wish to see that the requirements of Regulation 13(2)(a) have been complied with and also ensure that all appropriate information is incorporated into the pre-tender health and safety plan.

Regulation 13(2)(b) covers the inclusion in the design of adequate information concerning any aspect of the project, structure or materials which may affect any person carrying out construction or cleaning work in or on the structure at any time.

This should be interpreted to also include maintenance, repair decommissioning and so on. Typical of the things that a designer may usefully identify are avoiding contacts with certain materials, ensuring safe working loads, the provision of lifting or securement aids and so on – in particular those hazards which the principal contractor is unlikely to foresee.

The designer needs particularly to anticipate the risks that the principal contractor needs to be aware of.

All such information should be brought to the attention of the planning supervisor for inclusion in the pre-tender health and safety plan and/or the health and safety file.

Regulation 13(2)(c) covers the need for close cooperation between multiple designers and with the planning supervisor.

This is obviously a question of good communications and coordination. Where there are separate design teams working simultaneously on different structures within a project, the potential for health and safety problems between the various structures is a real possibility.

This means that there needs to be overall coordination to ensure that such things as an agreed set of design information and criteria are consistent across the design. In this respect, the planning supervisor needs to be closely involved and should attend key design meetings and discussions in order to ensure that appropriate information is included in the pre-tender health and safety plan and/or the health and safety file.

The principal contractor

Under the Regulations, the principal contractor has many health and safety-related duties to perform, including a number that fall under the 'Management of Health and Safety at Work Regulations' and other site-related regulations (see Regulation 16(1)(a)). Many of these are listed in general terms below. Where the numbers of the applicable Regulations are given, these and any support ACOP should be referred to if you need a more precise interpretation. The principal contractor will be a contractor by profession (see Regulation 6(2)) and will have demonstrated to the client both the competence and resources needed to carry out the duties entailed (see Regulation 16 and Regulations 8(3) and 9(3)).

Regulation 16

A construction health and safety plan will not be effective until it has been communicated to, and understood by, everyone on site.

A prime duty of the principal contractor is to develop and ensure the implementation of the health and safety plan. This is a vital document in which identified risks and the measures to be taken to address them are defined, including those relating to training, inter-party cooperation, surveillance and so on.

The requirements of the plan need to be properly communicated, understood, implemented, monitored and recorded. Ensuring that these things happen is a key duty of the principal contractor.

A further duty is to take reasonable steps to ensure cooperation between all contractors in order to enable each to comply with the requirements and prohibitions imposed by or under relevant statutory provisions relating to the construction work (see Regulation 16(1)(a).

By virtue of Regulation 3 of the Management of Health and Safety at Work Regulations 1999, all contractors are required to carry out risk assessments. The principal contractor will carry out his own risk assessments, as well as examine the implications of similar assessments carried out by other contractors. Where a common risk is apparent, the principal contractor will initiate a single risk assessment on behalf of those affected.

The health and safety plan is a vehicle for identifying risk situations and for communicating how to deal with them.

Other areas where a coordinated and cooperative approach are indicated include:

- health surveillance (Regulation 6 of MHSWR)
- health and safety assistance (Regulation 7 of MHSWR)
- procedures for serious and imminent danger and danger areas (Regulation 8 of the above Regulations)
- use of common equipment.

The principal contractor will also ensure that suitable arrangements for the above are established, communicated to contractors and employees, incorporated in the health and safety plan and (so far as is reasonable) are complied with (see Regulation 16(1)(b)).

A further duty is to ensure that a health and safety plan is made available for the client's (or client's representative's) acceptance *before* construction work is due to begin and that construction does *not* begin without this acceptance.

Regulation 16(1)(c) requires that the principal contractor shall take reasonable steps to ensure that only authorized persons gain access to premises (or parts thereof) where construction is being carried out.

The measures taken to meet this requirement are likely to vary depending on the size of the site, but would include identifying who is authorized, recognizing possible 'right of way' or access needs to adjacent areas, taking into account other contractors' individual controls and so on.

Again, the measures you take need to be established and defined within the health and safety plan.

As detailed earlier, one of the duties of the planning supervisor, under Regulation 7, is to notify the HSE with project information as required under Schedule 1. It is the duty of the principal contractor to ensure that the details given in this notification are displayed in a readable condition in a position where they can be read by anyone at work on construction work in connection with the project (see Regulation 16(1)(d)).

However, *it is not sufficient just to display this information*, the principal contractor needs to ensure that all contractors are aware of the contents. At the very least, the notice should be posted at various strategic locations around the site.

Regulation 16(1)(e) (i) (ii) and (iii) concerns the obligations of the principal contractor to provide the planning supervisor promptly with any information which the principal contractor has ascertained (or could ascertain by making reasonable enquiries) and which it is reasonable to believe the planning supervisor does not possess but should be included in the health and safety file.

Regulation 16(2) concerns the principal contractor's power to give directions to any contractor so that the principal contractor can comply with their duties under the Regulations, or to include in the health and safety plan rules for construction work which are reasonably required for health and safety purposes.

Regulation 16(3) takes the further step of requiring that any rules contained in the health and safety plan are to be in writing and brought to the attention of those affected by them.

This is a very clear duty on the principal contractor.

Regulation 17

There are further significant duties to be met under Regulations 17(1) and 17(2). Regulation 17(1) concerns the provision of comprehensive information on health and safety risks to every contractor or any employee or other persons under the control of that contractor, arising out of or in connection with the construction work.

This indicates a need for contractors to be given the relevant information from the health and safety plan, which in turn needs to be comprehensive and easily understandable.

Regulation 17(2) places upon the principal contractor the duty (insofar that it is reasonably practicable) of ensuring every contractor who is an employer provides health and safety information (as required under Regulation 10 of the MHSWR 1999) to their employees who are carrying out construction work, and also to provide any health and safety training which such an employer is required to provide (under Regulation 13(2)(b) of the same Regulations). How the principal contractor will ensure that the requirements of Regulation 17(2) have been met will vary, but examination of information distribution lists and training records, direct tests of understanding and verification by audits are a few typical measures.

Remember that some people on site may not have English as their first language or may be illiterate. Have they been made aware of the key parts of your health and safety plan?

It is important that the above steps under Regulations 17(1) and 17(2) take place before construction begins.

Note that it is one thing to have a comprehensive written health and safety plan but it is people's understanding of that plan and the way they carry it out that will help produce healthy and safe outcomes.

Regulation 18

Finally under Regulation 18(a) and (b) there is a provision that the principal contractor ensures that others (employees and self-employed persons) are able to discuss and offer project-related advice concerning health and safety matters and that their views can be coordinated as necessary for the greater benefit of health and safety.

We regard this as very important. There is a vast amount of 'coal-face' knowledge concerning health and safety working practices, and everyone should be encouraged to share this knowledge.

The contractor

The contractor will be a contractor by profession and will have demonstrated the necessary competence and resources to carry out their duties under the Regulations (see Regulations 8(3) and 9(3)). The duties of the contractor are essentially defined in Regulation 19 and are, in many cases, similar to those of the principal contractor.

The essence of Regulation 19 concerns close cooperation with the principal contractor, helping him to do his job and using the information and direction provided by and through him to do yours.

This is expressed in Regulation 19(1)(a) which requires co-operation with the principal contractor to the degree necessary to enable each party to comply with their duties under statutory provisions.

Cooperation obviously can take many forms. These include providing information (see Regulation 19(1)(b)), reacting to the information provided – for example, by circulating information to employees, providing selective training and so on – and providing information needed by the principal contractor in order to enable him to comply with his duties under the Regulations.

Regulation 19(1)(b) requires the contractor (so far as is reasonably practicable) to provide the principal contractor promptly with any information, including any relevant part of any risk assessment which may affect the health and safety of any person at work.

Contractors are expected to be well aware of risks associated with their normal work and with proven methods for countering such risks. However, there are other risks which may be identified within the health and safety plan, so it is important that all risks are identified and measures to combat them established. Everyone who could be affected needs to be made fully aware, and trained if necessary, and the principal contractor should be advised of both risks and measures being taken (including training, information circulation and so on) to counter them.

This will allow the principal contractor to assess the adequacy of such measures; to consider any wider implications and the possible need for a more inclusive risk assessment to be made.

It is a further duty of the contractor under Regulation 19(1)(c) to comply with any directions given to them by the principal contractor under Regulation 16(2)(a).

Regulation 19(1)(d) requires compliance with any applicable rules within the health and safety plan. Such rules, which the principal contractor is required to bring to the attention of the contractor, will need to be shared with every employee or self-employed person under the contractor's control. Taken together, Regulations 19(2), 19(3) and 19(4) require that no employer should cause or permit any employee of his, or any self-employed person to work on construction unless the employee or self-employed person has been provided with:

- the name of the planning supervisor for the project
- the name of the principal contractor for the project
- the contents of the health and safety plan or such part of it as is relevant to the construction that the employee or self-employed person is to undertake.

Regulations 19(1)(e) and 19(1)(f) are both concerned with the contractor's duty to provide information to the principal contractor. In the case of Regulation 19(1)(e), this covers information about any death, injury, condition or dangerous occurrence which is reportable under the Reporting of Injuries, Diseases and Dangerous Occurrence Regulations 1985.

Regulation 19(1)(f) is almost a reword of Regulation 16(1)(e) which describes the principal contractor's duty to pass information to the planning supervisor. However, in this case, the Regulation covers information from the contractor to the principal contractor.

Information that needs to be passed promptly to the principal contractor includes information:

- in the possession of the contractor (or which they could ascertain by way of reasonable enquiries to persons under their control)
- that they would reasonably believe that the principal contractor should provide to the planning supervisor in order to meet their obligations under Regulation 16(1)(e)
- which is not in the possession of the principal contractor.

This duty suggests the need for contractors to liaise closely with the principal contractor to discuss what is needed, available or could be reasonably ascertained, and also its purpose (for example, inclusion in the health and safety file).

Check (formally) that people have received and understood key health and safety information.

Regulation 19(5) concerns evidence that the information that you need to pass to employees and self-employed persons, prior to their being allowed to work on construction (see Regulations 19(2), 19(3) and 19(4)), has in fact been given to them. This evidence should be in the form of a formal record of receipt.

Integrating CDM requirements into the QMS

In Chapter 1 we emphasized that the QMS was not some 'add-on' to other business systems within an organization, but that it was, in fact, the management system of the business.

Later, in Chapter 12, we discuss the growing trend toward establishing integrated management systems. Incorporating the requirements of your duties under the CDM Regulations into your QMS is one step in this direction. How difficult it is to do this will obviously depend on the role played by your organization – for example, are you a client, design organization, design and build organization or contractor?

Whatever your type of organization, we trust that you already have in place a formal QMS. If you do not yet have one, the following guidance may not be immediately relevant, but it will become useful if and when a decision to introduce a QMS is taken.

Some organizations have attempted to introduce a single procedure entitled the 'CDM Regulations' or similar. The problem with a single-procedure approach is the tendency to end up with a list of things to be done, without giving real visibility to the 'how', 'when' and 'by whom'. As we have already said, health and safety matters are too important to rely purely on variable individual approaches.

Health and safety matters are too important for you to rely purely on variable individual approaches.

Consider for a moment just one duty that most parties have to perform, namely to carry out risk assessments:

- Who is to be involved in such assessments?
- What particular skills, qualifications and levels of seniority do those involved require?
- When are such assessments to be carried out? For example:
  - prior to work commencing?
  - during the work phase if significant changes (say, to a design) take place?
- Who initiates and controls the assessment?
- How are risk situations identified? For example:
  - by traditional knowledge and experience.
  - by reference to the health and safety plan
  - other.
- What techniques are used? For example:
  - assessment of potential consequences.
  - estimate of frequency of occurrence.
  - multiplying the above to determine a categorization, indicating the need for a specific level of action.
- Do considerations take into account and give priority to those situations which represent a risk to the many as opposed to the few?

- How are assessment results recorded? For example:
  - in reports
  - in minutes of meetings
  - other.
- Do these define both foreseen risk and proposed actions?
- Who is responsible for authorizing, distributing and recording outputs?
- Are any standard forms used?
- Are there circulation distribution lists or similar?
- Who approves the adequacy of proposed actions (for example, principal contractor)?
- Who ensures the incorporation of information into the health and safety plan and/or health and safety file?

The list of questions above is not necessarily definitive, although it is indicative of issues that need to be addressed in any decent procedure on the subject of risk assessments. The impact of this one procedure, however, has still wider implications within the QMS. The following are a few examples:

- The need for timely assessments should be included in work-related programmes.
- Reviews such as 'design reviews' need to ensure that assessments have been done, findings reacted to and information releases made to others, such as the planning supervisor.
- The assessment procedure itself needs to be identified within the relevant project quality plan (PQP), the monitoring of which will again confirm events such as implementation, results acceptance and information distribution.
- Copies of information will be incorporated in project records, the health and safety plan and so on.
- Audit checklists will make provision for reviews of procedure effectiveness.

All the above relate to only one subject. Nevertheless it does illustrate the likely shortcomings of a single all-embracing procedure approach.

We will now look a little more closely at the likely impact upon the QMS of the various parties whom we discussed earlier.

The following are abbreviated notes based on information to be found in *Addressing CDM Regulations through Quality Management Systems* written by one of the co-authors of this book.

The client's QMS

We will look at this on three levels, namely the 'policy statement', the organization charts and their supporting texts and, finally, certain procedures which may be affected.

The policy statement

This should contain words reflecting the importance that the organization places on health and safety matters, whether carried out 'in-house' or by others acting upon its behalf. It should also make it clear that these considerations embrace everything from conceptual design right through to the needs for maintenance and cleaning of the finished facility.

Health and safety policy needs to cover the design, construction, maintenance and cleaning of a structure.

Organization and responsibilities

You will recall that, earlier in this chapter, we identified four main duties of the client. How are these likely to affect the above?

If an agent is to be appointed to undertake the client's duties:

- Who makes the decision, when and on what basis?
- Is there a selection process that establishes the suitability of a potential agent, based on factors such as:
  - understanding of the client's role and duties
  - the necessary ability to evaluate and appoint others
  - interface responsibilities
  - resources and competence
  - supplying information to the planning supervisor
  - confirming the adequacy of the health and safety plan
  - awareness of duties with respect to the purpose, receipt and control of the health and safety file.
- If not, how can confidence be demonstrated?

If the client is to be directly responsible:

- Who is responsible for appointments such as planning, supervisor, designer, principal contractor and so on?
- What methods are used to predetermine the suitability of appointees – for example, 'preferred lists'?
- Who is responsible for collating and providing project-related information to the planning supervisor?
- Who is responsible for the review and acceptance of health and safety plans?
- Who ensures that the positions of planning supervisor and principal contractor remain filled throughout the life of the project?
- Who is responsible for the receipt, maintenance and control of the health and safety file?

All the above responsibilities should be clearly defined within the organization structure.

We also suggest that, because the planning supervisor is directly responsible to the client, the two positions should be linked by a dotted line on any project organization chart.

Procedures

A number of these are likely to need minor adjustment, as follows:

1 **Procedure concerning the appointment of others**

   These will include:
   - selection of suitable appointees
   - invitations to tender
   - bid appraisal
   - appointments.

   With respect to these, you will need to define the following:
   - the basis of selecting appointees (for example, through using preferred lists, completed questionnaires, track records and so on)
   - evaluation criteria (that is, factors considered)
   - inclusions of special clauses within tender invitations relating to QMS and health and safety requirements
   - selection routines
   - the preparation of appointment documentation (including any special QMS or health and safety-related requirements)
   - notifications to unsuccessful bidders
   - formal appointment
   - monitoring post-appointment performances (including health and safety activity-related performance)
   - actions taken as a result of performance monitoring (for example, revision of preferred lists)
   - reference to documentation used (for example, standard forms)
   - records to be retained
   - responsibilities associated with the above actions.

2 **Procedures concerning the establishment and updating of preferred supplier lists or similar**

   The procedure should be reviewed to ensure that health and safety considerations are included as a basis of qualification, along with those relating to financial stability, technical ability, quality management and availability of resources.

   The procedure should make it clear what qualifying criteria are used to gain inclusion on to the list(s) – for example, the completion of an appropriate questionnaire, track record, reliable recommendations of others and so on.

   It should be apparent:
   - who compiles and controls the list(s)
   - how performances are reviewed, by whom, how often and actions resulting
   - what documentation is used

Before you appoint suppliers, you need to vet their health and safety procedures, just as you vet the quality of their past work and their ability to deliver on the current project.

- what records are held and what access limitations apply.

3 Procedures concerning the preparation of project information for passing to the planning supervisor

An example of the information required has been given under 'The Client (or Appointed Agent Acting as the Client)' p. 82.

The procedure should define:
- The purpose of the information
- who prepares the information
- methods used (for example, the generation of information through a group of knowledgeable people as opposed to simply through an individual)
- timing and delivery to the planning supervisor
- formats used
- authorization
- records.

4 Procedures defining the levels of quality management required

Up until the introduction of ISO 9001:2000 it was possible to define the levels of quality management by equating QM requirements to appropriate parts of the prevailing standard, using statements in tender invitation and contract documents such as 'The supplier shall carry out his assigned duties in accordance with the requirements of ISO 9001, ISO 9002 or ISO 9003', (deleting whichever were not applicable).

Your qualifying criteria should help you select preferred suppliers.

Under ISO 9001:2000 (and following the withdrawal of the old ISO 9002 and 9003) you need to express your requirements by exception, stating those parts of the standard which are pertinent (for example, if a job entailed no design work whatsoever, then section 7.3 of the standard would not directly apply).

Once established, the QM criteria become an input to any tender invitation and contract documentation, and they should help you select suitable organizations from any preferred list.

The procedure should describe how such requirements are established, when, and by whom and how they are recorded.

5 Procedures for training

Any procedure on this subject should be reviewed to ensure that training encompasses the client's duties under the CDM Regulations.

6 Procedures for quality plans

If the client uses quality plans to help monitor project activities, these should reflect their own key health and safety-related duties and their timings.

7 **Procedures for auditing**

If the client carries out their own programme of project audits, any checklists developed for these should monitor health and safety-related activities and adherence to their implementing procedures.

8 **Procedures for the health and safety file**

This should be the subject of a stand-alone procedure, which will cover:
- purpose
- required format
- interfaces with planning supervisor
- responsibilities for information receipt, contents check, safe keeping, access controls, information release controls and records including the reasons for such releases.

9 **Procedures for management review**

The management review should be included procedures for reviewing the effectiveness of the organization's health and safety policy, strategies and the meeting of requirements laid down by the CDM Regulations.

The planning supervisor's QMS

We will now consider the likely effects upon the QMS of an organization offering the service of planning supervisor.

The policy statement

See the comments made earlier with respect to the client's QMS (p. 94).

Organization and responsibilities

We suggest that the position of planning supervisor on any organization chart should show a direct reporting link to the client.

Any associated descriptive text should make it clear that the planning supervisor is directly responsible to the client for carrying out the specific health and safety-related duties as defined in the CDM Regulations and enjoys the full operational independence and freedom to do so.

Procedures

1 **Procedures for contract review or equivalent**

Although the duties of the planning supervisor are clearly defined under the CDM Regulations, the degree to which they apply may vary depending on the client's ability and/or decision to do certain things directly. For example, the client may seek the planning supervisor's advice on the suitability of potential appointees for other roles, in which case the planning supervisor would have a wider role to play, than if the client decided that their own selection procedures were fully adequate.

It is essential therefore to establish the precise degree of support needed on a project-by-project basis and then to determine and confirm the actual competences and resources needed.

Different clients will need different levels of support and it's up to the planning supervisor to establish what's appropriate for each project.

Draft a list of all the possible duties that might be required of the planning supervisor and use it as a checklist to help you ascertain the client's precise requirements. This is the only way in which you will be able to arrive at a realistic fee estimate, which is likely to be the basis on which the contract will be awarded.

2 Procedures for reviews of the preparation, update and control of work programmes, such as networks

The planning supervisor will wish to ensure that work programmes identify health and safety-related activities and that such activities (for example, risk assessments) are not only being properly implemented, verified and acted upon, but also that appropriate information is incorporated into the pre-tender health and safety plan and included in the health and safety file. This is particularly important in relation to design activities.

3 Procedures for notifying project information to the HSE (see HSE form F10)

You need to establish a procedure or instruction defining:
- information required
- timing
- format
- records
- distributions (for example, the principal contractor in order to enable them to comply with their obligations under Regulation 16(1)(d)).

4 Procedures for preparing pre-tender health and safety plan

This duty has only come into being since the position of planning supervisor was created. It is a requirement that the planning supervisor *ensures* that a health and safety plan has been prepared, prior to invitations to tender being sent out. This does not mean, however, that the planning supervisor has to prepare the plan personally (although this may often be the case). It is suggested that a procedure or instruction be produced, addressing:
- how the planning supervisor *does* ensure the adequacy of such a plan

- what information should be included
- what evidence of health and safety considerations are sought
- how the plan is generated
- what information inputs are made (for example, project information supplied by the client)
- who produces the information
- what format is used
- who authorizes the plan
- who controls its distribution

and so on.

The above is by no means a complete list. However, the benefits of having a procedure which cross-references a list of these points will far outweigh the benefits to be had from individual interpretations or those based on 'What did you cover?' type discussions with others.

5 Procedures for the health and safety file

It is the planning supervisor's duty to *ensure* that a health and safety file is compiled for each structure. Although the file will largely be compiled by others (for example, the principal contractor), it is the planning supervisor's responsibility to ensure that this is an ongoing process and that, by the end of the construction phase, the file(s) is (are) complete and suitable for handover to the client.

The presentation of the file may vary; it could be a compilation of a number of files each relating to discrete structures. We suggest that you establish a dedicated procedure for the health and safety file, addressing the following:

- the planning supervisor's responsibilities for ensuring compilation and control
- the file's contents
- agreement with the client (if necessary) concerning the preferred structure and format of the file
- liaison with others about what information to include
- where the file is to be kept and who may access it
- a check, prior to handover, to make sure the file is complete
- safekeeping and access controls pending transfer to the client
- handover to the client.

6 Procedures for management review

Although it is unlikely that a planning supervisor will be directly involved in a management review, it would neverthe-less be useful if they could make an objective and informed input on the effectiveness or otherwise of the health and safety policy and measures, if asked.

7 **Procedures for selection and appointment of support services**

You need to review any procedure for selecting and appointing support services to ensure that the basis on which any appointments are decided fully reflect the client's expectations (see Chapter 8).

8 **Procedures for document control/distribution lists**

These should be reviewed to ensure that requirements under the CDM Regulations are catered for – for example:
 - notifications to the HSE
 - receipt and ongoing distribution of project information from the client
 - receipt and handover of the health and safety file and so on.

9 **Procedures for training**

All organizations within the construction industry should include, within their training programmes, details of relevant implications of the CDM Regulations for their staff, including those concerning relationships with the planning supervisor.

10 **Procedures for internal audits**

Although the role of planning supervisor is independent of mainstream activities, any organization providing such services should monitor their effectiveness as part of its auditing function. Any audit checklists used should make provision for this.

11 **Procedures for quality plans**

Any procedures operated by other parties (for example, the designer or the principal contractor) concerning the preparation and use of quality plans should require that such plans include all distributions and so on needed by the planning supervisor, who in turn should advise which copies of design documents they would like to receive or any meetings they would like to attend.

The designer's QMS

The design organization has some foreseeable effects on the QMS, and these are considered below.

The policy statement

This should be reviewed to ensure that it adequately reflects recognition of health and safety requirements under the Regulations.

Organization and responsibilities

Relevant charts and supporting texts should be reviewed to make it clear who carries out specific responsibilities under CDM Regulation 13, such as:

- alerting the client to their duties under the Regulations
- key liaisons with others, such as the planning supervisor and principal contractor.

If the organization is offering the services of a planning supervisor, this position should be shown on the appropriate organization chart and the accompanying text should describe such key details as follows:

- The role may be filled only by suitable persons who are fully conversant with their duties under the CDM Regulations.
- The planning supervisor is directly accountable to the client.
- The planning supervisor has the freedom to operate in an impartial manner.
- The role is a stand-alone appointment and, as such, is subject to a separate fee arrangement.

and so on.

It is also useful to include in this section of the quality manual a few words about how the health and safety policy is in fact implemented – that is, suitably qualified and experienced staff carrying out risk assessments aimed at determining potential risks associated with materials and methods of construction, the actual construction proper, maintenance, cleaning and so on. This should be followed by a brief summary of how the risk assessment findings lead to the elimination of risks (where possible) through design changes or (if not possible) by ensuring that others are made fully aware of any remaining risks.

Procedures

1 **Procedures for contract review**

Any procedure concerning the pre-consideration of the work to be undertaken should include confirmation that duties under the Regulations are fully understood and can be resourced.

2 **Procedures for work programming**

Any procedure concerning work programming should include all health and safety-related activities – for example, key meetings with others, risk assessments, the issue of safety-related information.

3 **Procedures for quality plans**

Quality plan procedures must ensure that health and safety documents, activities, records and distributions are visibly included and monitored.

4 **Procedures for the control of design base documents (technical library)**

Any procedure concerning this subject should ensure that health and safety documents are incorporated. This should include the CDM Regulations, associated ACOPs and so on.

Setting up a dedicated section within the technical library for health and safety-related documents will make finding and referring to these materials much easier.

A well-organized technical library makes accessing important health and safety documents much easier.

5 **Procedures for design review**

Design reviews should have procedures for reviewing the implementation of health and safety activities, such as timely notifications to others, risk assessments and associated actions and inputs from the planning supervisor.

6 **Procedures for internal audits**

Checklists for such audits should include coverage of health and safety activities.

7 **Procedures for risk assessments**

The procedures for risk assessment should make it clear not only how such assessments are planned and conducted, but also how the results are communicated to others, what formats are used, timing, responsibility for the doing and how the records are retained.

8 **Procedures for training**

Make sure that training procedures cover:
  – responsibilities under the Regulations
  – risk assessments
  – safety-related liaisons with others, particularly the planning supervisor
  – use of (and input to, if appropriate) the health and safety database.

9 **Procedures for management review**

Management review procedures should make positive provision for the ongoing adequacy and effectiveness of the organization's health and safety policy and strategies.

10 **Procedures for quality records**

Quality records should include all records generated as a result of the Regulations.

The principal contractor's QMS

The policy statement

This should be reviewed and include reference to the fact that it is the organization's policy to ensure the safety of its staff or others working on its behalf on construction work in accordance with the CDM Regulations. It should also state that activities are conducted in accordance with the Regulations and with pre-identified health and safety arrangements that have been accepted by the client and are defined within a dynamic health and safety plan.

Organization and responsibilities

Because of the many duties which fall to the principal contractor under the CDM Regulations, this section of an organization's manual may need some significant additions, particularly with respect to the responsibilities for the following:

- developing the health and safety plan
- ensuring that the relevant parts of the health and safety plan are distributed to others
- liaison with the planning supervisor
- pre-appointment assessments of the health and safety, and health surveillance, arrangements of support contractors
- a check and pre-construction submission of the health and safety plan(s) for client acceptance
- chairing health and safety-related meetings
- building up information for the health and safety file
- ensuring that adequate arrangements for cooperation between others are established
- ensuring the safe use of mutually shared equipment
- posting site notices containing the required information about notifiable projects.

Your manual needs to make it clear (by job function and name) who has responsibility for each of these areas.

Procedures

1 **Procedures for management review**

   Health and safety policy and strategies should be included within a formal and ongoing agenda for management reviews.

2 **Procedures for contract review**

   The contract review, or equivalent procedure equating capability and resources to project needs, should be studied to ensure that it includes:

- study of the pre-tender health and safety plan provided by the planning supervisor
- the numerous duties with respect to the coordination and cooperation of other contractors
- opportunities for carrying out mutual risk assessments
- ensuring site safety measures
- chairing health and safety meetings and so on.

Draw up a list identifying all foreseeable duties under the Regulations, and then (in conjunction with the brief received and the pre-tender health and safety plan) use the list to conduct the review. The planning supervisor should be able to clarify unclear situations as needed.

3 Procedures for project programmes

Any such programmes should include:
- risk assessments
- review of contractor assessments, appraising contractor health surveillance and emergency measures
- developing the health and safety plan and the timely submission of the same for pre-construction acceptance by the client
- posting of site notices
- key meetings

and so on.

4 Procedures for preferred supplier list(s)

Any procedure for preparing preferred supplier lists should be reviewed to ensure that the evaluation criteria include those relating to health and safety capability.

5 Procedures for tender invitations

Any procedure for inviting tenders should ensure that health and safety requirements are fully defined: for example, make sure that you include relevant parts of the health and safety plan.

6 Procedures for bid appraisals

Any procedure for bid appraisals should ensure a detailed evaluation of responses to health and safety issues and a further elaboration of such responses when necessary.

7 Procedures for quality plans

Any procedure relating to the preparation and use of quality plans should ensure that the following are included:
- responsibilities for carrying out health and safety-related activities
- the identification of important health and safety-related documents, such as the health and safety plan, risk assessment reports and so on
- the nature and timing of key safety-related meetings

- the timings of submissions to others (for example, of the health and safety plan to the client for preconstruction acceptance)
- key communication routes between the various parties
- audit and review stages
- records requirements.

8 **Procedures for feedback**

Any feedback procedures (from any source, whether internal or external) should encourage people to offer information relating to health and safety performance.

9 **Procedures for the control of work-based documents**

Ensure that any procedure concerning work-based documents requires the inclusion of health and safety-related documents, such as the CDM Regulations, supporting ACOPs and so on.

10 **Procedures for non-conformance/preventive actions**

Review such procedures and, if necessary, build in special measures to identify and process health and safety-related situations.

11 **Procedures for the control of inspection, measuring and test equipment**

Ensure that any procedure for the calibration and use of such equipment(s) includes any instruments or other tools used for safety-related purposes.

12 **Procedures for internal audits**

Ensure that checklists established for such audits include verification of the proper understanding and implementation of health and safety-related activities as required by the Regulations.

13 **Procedures for purchasing (including services)**

Ensure that any purchasing procedures include all health and safety-related guidance and requirements – for example, extracts from the health and safety plan.

14 **Procedures for training**

Any procedures for training need to include all relevant health and safety matters. Evidence of such training should also be recorded.

15 **Procedures for records**

These procedures should include all significant health and safety-related documents, such as the health and safety plan, communications with the planning supervisor, minutes of meetings, assessment reports and so on.

16 Procedures for health surveillance

Ensure that any procedure allows for coordination with other parties' arrangements.

17 Procedures for risk assessments

As with health surveillance, ensure that any procedure allows for coordination with other parties' arrangements.

The contractor's QMS

The policy statement

The policy statement should be reviewed to ensure that it includes a positive commitment to health and safety.

Organization and responsibilities

The manual should be reviewed to ensure that the previously described duties of the contractor are equated to the people responsible for their enactment. These would include:

- reviewing the health and safety plan
- conveying requirements of this plan to others
- liaising with the principal contractor concerning matters such as:
  - health surveillance
  - emergency procedures
  - mutually shared equipment
  - passing on information.

Procedures

1 Procedures for management review

Check to see if your management review procedures make adequate provision for review of the health and safety policy and its implementation.

2 Procedures for contract review

Ensure that your contract review procedures make provision for all health and safety duties to be undertaken and take into full consideration any requirements of the health and safety plan.

3 Procedures for selection and appointment

Ensure that:
- selection procedures cover the candidate's/organization's health and safety capabilities
- health and safety requirements to be met are fully included within any tender invitations

- bid appraisals include checks for the adequacy and understanding of health and safety matters and the capability to meet them
- health and safety requirements are incorporated into contract documents
- evaluations of ongoing health and safety-related performances are made.

4 Procedures for work programmes

Any procedure on this subject should require the inclusion of all key health and safety-related activities.

5 Procedures for quality plans

As with work programmes, procedures, all key quality-related meetings, reviews, document distributions, special training needs, liaisons, records and so on should be incorporated.

6 Procedures for calibration

Ensure that any procedure for the calibration and use of equipment includes any instruments or other tools used for safety-related purposes.

7 Procedures for internal audits

Ensure that the checklists established for such audits include verification of the proper understanding and implementation of health and safety-related activities as required by the Regulations.

8 Procedures for records

Procedures for records should require all health and safety-related documents, such as minutes of meetings, training information and liaisons with principal contractor, be included.

9 Procedures for training

As for other parties, any programme should include training in duties relating to the Regulations, as well as relevant aspects of the health and safety plan.

10 Procedures for work-based documents

Health and safety-related standards, regulations, supporting ACOPs and other key documents should all be included within the compass of any control procedure.

Chapter **7**

Project Quality Plans

Purpose

Project quality plans (PQPs) have been used extensively in the construction industry for the past 20 years. They first came to prominence on large construction projects relating to the nuclear industry and petro-chemical industries, but have since spread to all sectors of construction.

A PQP consists of documents which are prepared using the organization's QMS, in a way that specifies the processes and associated resources to be used to help manage and control a package of work.

Within the industry there is a degree of confusion between what in some sectors are known as 'quality programmes' and PQPs. In essence they are the same thing – mini QMSs which identify the following for a specific project:

- the organization and responsibilities
- work planning/programmes
- processes
- regulations
- standards
- implementing procedures
- interface and record requirements.

A subordinate document, which may also be referenced within a PQP, is a detail quality plan (DQP), which is ideal for describing the controls for a discrete, but perhaps significant, piece of work or set of activities within the project, where very close controls are indicated.

The differences between, and uses of, PQPs and DQPs are described below.

The project quality plan (PQP)

This document will typically include:

- project title
- project number
- name of project manager
- a description of the scope of work
- a project-specific organizational chart and supporting responsibility text
- a statement of interface involvements and limitations between your own organization and other parties – for example, the client, consultant, planning supervisor, principal contractor, regulating bodies and so on
- communication links

- reference to all relevant procedures or other controlling documents – for example, in the case of an architectural practice, the applicable work stages from the *RIBA Job Book*
- reference to specific contract requirements – for example, standards, regulations, codes of practice, client deliverables and so on
- a list of any project-related work packages for which DQPs are to be prepared
- a schedule of any intended audits to be carried out
- a list of utilities, local authorities and so on, which need to be contacted
- reference to the programmes to be prepared – for example, networks or resource programmes
- a statement regarding what records are to be produced, how they are to be compiled during the life of the project – for example, hard copy or electronic or both – and where they are to be located.

This is not a definitive list of requirements and will vary according to the scope of the project. Such plans are tailored directly to cover the demands of the work in question and are therefore a unique statement of the management and control arrangements for the particular project.

The main advantages of PQPs are as follows:

As long as you have a formal QMS, PQPs should be easy to prepare.

1   They are easy and quick to prepare provided that you have a formal QMS from which to select the applicable procedures and other control documents.
2   Because they involve reviewing and including the client's scope of work, the chances of missing any important aspect are reduced, especially if the client expresses the wish to approve the document before work starts.
3   They are the key ongoing references for the management and control of project activities.

A typical example or outline of such a plan submitted at the tender stage can indicate both a good understanding of job requirement and an ability to manage the work in a competent manner, and can also prove helpful in providing the tenderer with a competitive edge.

Remember that the tender stage is the most important; failure at this stage means no contract.

PQPs should be structured in such a manner that they promote your QMS capability and demonstrate your understanding of, and ability to, effectively manage the work in question.

Figures 7.1, 7.2 and 7.3 show the first three pages from a typical PQP. They are followed by examples of what to include in the various sections, based on the index shown in Figure 7.3.

```
┌─────────────────────────────────────────────────────────────┐
│ ABB Design                              Issue 1               │
│                                                              │
│          Project Quality Plan           Page 1 of            │
│                                                              │
│ Title:   Design and construction of the West Island         │
│          Warehouse at Mancuster                              │
│                                                              │
│ Prepared By:              Signature:         Date:          │
│ Name:                                                        │
│ P. Sumner                                                    │
│ (Senior Designer)                                            │
│                                                              │
│ Approved For Issue By:    Signature:         Date:          │
│ B. Thorpe                                                    │
│ (Project Manager)                                            │
│                                                              │
│                                                              │
│ Copy Number:                                                │
│                                                              │
│ Project reference no.                                        │
│ AB/1256/03                                                   │
└─────────────────────────────────────────────────────────────┘
```

Figure 7.1 *Typical project quality plan front sheet*

```
┌─────────────────────────────────────────────────────────────┐
│ ABB Design                              Issue 1               │
│                                                              │
│          Project Quality Plan           Page 2 of            │
│                                                              │
│  Distribution:                                               │
│                                                              │
│  B Devine          Client – Mancuster CC                    │
│  P. Sumner         Senior Designer – ABB                    │
│  B. Thorpe         Project Manager – ABB                    │
│  L. Jones          Planning Engineer – ABB                  │
│  L. Sweet          Quality Engineer – ABB                   │
│  I. Spy            Planning Supervisor – C & DM Ltd         │
│                                                              │
│  History Sheet:                                             │
│                                                              │
│  Issue Number:     Comment:             Date:              │
│                                                              │
│  1st draft                                                  │
│                                                              │
│                                                              │
│  Project reference no.                                      │
│  AB/1256/03                                                 │
└─────────────────────────────────────────────────────────────┘
```

Figure 7.2 *Typical project quality plan distribution*

```
┌─────────────────────────────────────────────────────────┐
│                                              Issue 1      │
│        Project Quality Plan Index                        │
│                                              Page 3 of    │
│  Contents                                                │
```

1	Introduction, Objectives and Policy	4
*	1.1 Introduction	4
*	1.2 Objectives	5
*	1.3 Policy statement	6
2	Scope	6
3	Organization and Responsibilities	6
	3.1 Staff charts/organization chart	6
	3.2 Project Interfaces	7
	3.3 Responsibilities	7
4	Project Information, Procedures, Work Packages and Detail Quality Plans (DQPs)	7
	4.1 Key meetings	7
	4.2 Key standards and regulations	7
	4.3 Interfacing bodies	7
	4.4 ABB procedures	8
	4.5 Work packages and DQPs	8
5	Records, Document and Data Control Processes, and Project Files	8
	5.1 Records	8
	5.2 Document and data control	8
	5.3 Project files	9
6	Contracted Services	9
7	Financial Control and Reporting	9
8	Safety	9
9	Audit Programme	10

Project reference no.
AB/1256/03

Note: Items marked * are essentially for client interest.

Figure 7.3 *Typical project quality plan index*

Section 1: Introduction, objectives and policy

- Give an introduction and brief description to the scheme (this could be an extract from the client's specification).
- Identify the objectives of the project (this, again, could be an extract from the client's specification).
- Include any reference to the applicable quality standard.

Section 2: Scope

- Describe the scope of work to be covered by this PQP (this could be an extract from the client's specification).

Section 3: Organization and responsibilities

- Show or reference a project-specific organizational chart with names of the key players. Clearly describe also the responsibilities of the individuals (extract information from the O & R section of your quality manual and customize it to suit the project requirements).
- Either on the same organizational chart or on a separate chart show the interfacing organizations (for example, client, planning supervisor, principal contractor and so on) with individual names and job titles (if appointed). It is important to show or describe what happens at the interfaces – that is, who speaks to whom and about what subjects. There should be very clear lines of communication.

A key requirement for a successful PQP is clear lines of communication.

Section 4: Project information

- **4.1 Key meetings**
  List the key meeting and the chairperson. For example:

Meeting	Chairperson
Monthly progress meeting with the client	Project manager
Monthly progress meeting with the principal contractor	Project manager
Meeting as requested with the planning supervisor	Project manager

- **4.2 Key standards and regulations**
  List the key standards and regulations.
  Where possible, identify these from the client's specification, plus others (for example, those relating to health and safety). In the same way as when you list procedures, make sure that you identify title, reference number and issue status.

- **4.3 Interfacing bodies**
  List the interfacing bodies. For example:
  - local planning authority (contact name and telephone number)
  - utilities (for example, electric, water and so on, as relevant)
  - client contact (name and contact number)
  - principal contractor (name and contact number)
  - planning supervisor (name and contact number)

- main contact on the site (name and contact number)
- others.

- **4.4 Company procedures**

  List the applicable in-house company procedure numbers and titles from the quality manual, together with their issue status, along with any specifically requested by the client (which may replace your own procedures). For example,

  - ABB/P/101 issue 1: Preparation and approval of drawings
  - ABB/P/102 issue 2: Preparation and approval of calculations
  - MCC/P/40 issue 1: Submission of Technical Queries (Client procedure)
  - MCC/F/TQ issue 1: Technical Query Form (Client form).

- **4.5 Work packages and DQPs**

  List the breakdown of work packages/tasks which make up the project. For example:

  - design of warehouse
  - construction of warehouse
  - design and installation of overhead crane.

  List the DQPs required:

  - design phase
  - foundations (from the chosen contractor)
  - structural steelwork design and erection (from the chosen contractor)
  - design and installation of overhead crane (from the chosen contractor)
  - design and installation of heating and ventilation system (from the chosen contractor).

Section 5: Records, document and data control processes, and project files

- **5.1 Records**

  - Define the control of records by referring to the control document (make reference to your QM procedure).
  - State what records you will deliver to the client or others, such as the planning supervisor. Alternatively, reference a document (for example, a plan) which defines such records).
  - Define where your company's records will be stored and for what period (some records may need to be stored for the lifetime of the structure).

- **5.2   Document and data control**
  Define the processes for storing documents and issuing them in a controlled manner to the client and others during the live project phase.

- **5.3   Project files**
  Define the file structure, the numbering system adopted, and whether paper or electronic or both is to be used.

Section 6: Contracted services

List the contracted services. In the construction industry these may be:

- overhead crane manufacture and installation
- erection of steelwork.

Section 7: Financial control and reporting

If it is a client requirement, define how you propose to report financial information to the client and at what frequency. For example, you may choose to provide a monthly cost flow statement to the client.

Section 8: Safety

Make reference to your safety manual or the safety procedures that will be employed on this contract, and how safety will be monitored.

Section 9: Audit programme

Define any internal programme of audits on this contract. For example:

Audit reference	Scope of audit	When
ABB/701	Design phase: • Check that risk assessments are complete and accepted by the planning supervisor. • Check that records are complete.	During the detail design phase
ABB/702	Construction phase: • Check that all stages are complete and records are available for the site activities including those for the health and safety file.	During the structural steel erection phase

The limitations of PQPs

One limitation of PQPs is that, although they define who is to do what, which procedures are to be applied and the management controls needed, there are occasionally situations when extra detailed controls are indicated. Where this is the case, another document that has been widely used in the manufacturing industry for many years and is now used, for the control of site activities in civil and structural work programme is appropriate. This document is the detail quality plan.

The detail quality plan (DQP)

The DQP is used to control activities on discrete packages of work, of which there may be many within the total scope of a project. Typical packages would relate to:

- designing a structure
- fabricating a structure
- sinking piles
- making reinforced concrete sections
- placement of cladding
- manufacture and installation of heating and ventilation systems.

A DQP fulfils four essential functions:

1   It demands prior consideration about the task to be undertaken, because it is necessary to read through all the relevant specifications, standards, instructions and so on so that the significant requirements can be restated in a different document (the DQP).
2   It allows those for whom the work is being done (such as the client or the project manager) to see in advance:
    – intended activities
    – responsibilities
    – verifications
    – information distributions and
    – records
to be generated at each stage, and to make any change requests if necessary.
3   It allows you to exercise visible controls at every stage of the work programme.
4   At the end of the project the signed-off DQP, along with the supporting documentation generated during implementation, provides a total record of satisfactory work completion.

Figure 7.4 show typical formats for the front sheet and the first two continuation sheets of a hypothetical DQP for the design phase of a project. Formats can vary from company to company.

Client:
Mancuster CC

Customer REF (Order No.)
Man/233333/03

CONTRACT DESCRIPTION:
Design and construction of the West Island Warehouse at Mancuster

ABB Project No:
ABB/1256/03

SCOPE OF DETAIL QUALITY PLAN:
Design phase – Design of West Island Warehouse

REASON FOR ISSUE/AMENDMENTS:
Issue 1 – For client approval

PREPARED BY: P. Sumner	DATE: 03/11/03	APPROVED BY:

FINAL SIGN OFF BY ABB.

NAME: B. Thorpe	SIGNATURE	DATE

FINAL SIGN OFF BY CLIENT

NAME	SIGNATURE	DATE

NOTES:

A   100% inspection
B   Document to be checked and approved by ABB
C   Document to be checked and approved by client
D   Document required for client records
E   Document for own records
F   Final inspection
H   Hold point
P   Documents to be issued to the planning supervisor

DISTRIBUTION

1 Client
2 Planning Supervisor
3
4
5
6
7
8

Prior to final signature:
All activities required by this quality plan have been carried out in accordance with the applicable controlling document and all records are available.

Detail Quality Plan	PLAN PREPARED BY: P. Sumner (ABB)	DATE: 03/11/03	QUALITY PLAN NO: ABB/209
ABB	PLAN APPROVED BY: B. Thorpe (ABB)	DATE: 10/11/03	ISSUE: 1
Designers	CLIENT ACCEPTANCE:	DATE:	Page 1 of 3

Form Ref: ABB DQP

ACTIVITY NO. (1)	ACTIVITY (2)	DEMANDING/ CONTROLLING DOCUMENT (3)	VERIFICATION (4)			IDENTIFIED RECORD/VERIFYING DOCUMENT (5)	ISSUED TO (6)		
			CODE	BY	DATE		CODE	SIG	DATE
1	Prepare DQP in accordance with client's specification and submit for approval	Spec. MANCC/12900 ABB/03	B	PM		This document	D, E		
2	Allocate drawing, project file and file references	ABB/P/106		Des		Drawing register and project filing system	E		
3	Agree technical queries	ABB/P/103		PM		Formal client response to TQs	D		
4	Carry out site survey	ABB/P/104	B	PM		Survey report	D, E		
5	Obtain copies of as-built drawing and safety-related information	ABB/P/104							
6	Notify client of his duties under the CDM Regulations	CDM Reg. 13				Copy of letter			
7	Prepare programme of work	ABB/P/105	B	PM		Authorized programmes	D, E		
8	Prepare calculations	ABB/P/102	B	Des		Verified calculations	D, E		
9	Prepare drawings	ABB/P/101	B	Des		Approved drawings	D. E		
10	Carry out design risk assessments and pass details to the planning supervisor for the pre-tender health and safety plan	ABB/P/111 CDM Reg. 13	B	Des		Risk assessment reports	E, P		

Page 2 of 3

Figure 7.4 Example front page and continuation sheets of a typical DQP (design phase) (Continued)

ACTIVITY NO. (1)	ACTIVITY (2)	DEMANDING/ CONTROLLING DOCUMENT (3)	VERIFICATION (4)			IDENTIFIED RECORD/VERIFYING DOCUMENT (5)	ISSUED TO (6)		
			CODE	BY	DATE		CODE	SIG	DATE
11	Carry out design review	ABB/P/112	B	PM		Design review minutes	D		
12	All activities on the DQP complete and all records available	Specification	F	PM		Fully signed off DQP	C, D, E		

Design phase of the West Island Warehouse at Mancuster

QUALITY PLAN NO: ABB/209

Page 3 of 3

Approval Codes: PM = Project Manager, Des = Designer

Figure 7.4 Concluded

It should be noted that the front sheet contains provision for acceptance/approval by the client or contracting authority for which the work is being undertaken, before work actually begins. This not only allows the client to see that specified requirements have been fully identified and planned for, but also allows for them to insert codes (see the bottom of the front sheet) indicating those stages where they wish to have direct involvement, receive records and so forth.

Activities are presented in sequential order:

- Column 1 shows the activity number.
- Column 2 describes the activity.
- Column 3 identifies the controlling document(s), which define(s) how the activity is to be carried out.
- Column 4 identifies the level of verification or control to be applied during the activity. This will be signified by one or more of the code numbers listed on sheet 1. These codes represent involvement by either or both parties to the contract who will append their signatures of stage acceptance when the activity in question is satisfactorily accomplished.
- Column 5 states what is to constitute evidence of the activity in column 2 being properly completed in accordance with the controls defined in column 3.
- Column 6 defines where the records identified in column 5 are required to be distributed – client, contractor, planning supervisor and so on. This information is usually expressed in the form of a code number as shown on sheet 1.

It is often possible to produce generic DQPs which can be used for different contracts because activities tend to be carried out in a standard sequence as, for example, with manufacture of pre-cast concrete blocks. It is then only necessary to alter details such as client name, contract number, product description and client involvement for each contract.

Figure 7.5 is an example of the front page and four continuation sheets of a DQP for the manufacturing phase of a project. It shows a DQP used by the 'Former Concrete Block Company' for submission to its client, Mancuster CC, for precast concrete blocks. This particular DQP is generic in nature, in that the same format of DQP can be followed when producing precast concrete blocks for other clients. See page 126 for procedure.

Client: Mancuster CC	Customer REF (Order No.) Man/244444/03		

CONTRACT DESCRIPTION:
Precast Blocks for Mancuster Sewage Works

Project No: FCBC/70/30

SCOPE OF DETAIL QUALITY PLAN:
Manufacture of Former Block 6

REASON FOR ISSUE/AMENDMENTS:
Issue 1 – For client approval

PREPARED BY: W. Done	DATE: 03/11/03	APPROVED BY:

FINAL SIGN OFF BY ABB.

NAME: B. Good	SIGNATURE	DATE

FINAL SIGN OFF BY CLIENT

NAME	SIGNATURE	DATE

NOTES:

A   Documentation submission
B   Client's approval
C   Records for client
F   Final inspection
H   Hold point
I   100% inspection
P   Sample inspection
R   Records for FCBC

DISTRIBUTION

1 Client
2
3
4
5
6
7
8

Prior to final signature:
All activities required by this quality plan have been carried out in accordance with the applicable controlling document and all records are available.

Detail Quality Plan	PLAN PREPARED BY: W. Done (FCBC)	DATE: 03/11/03	QUALITY PLAN NO: FCBC/62
FCBC	PLAN APPROVED BY: B. Good (FCBC)	DATE: 10/11/03	ISSUE: 1
	CLIENT ACCEPTANCE:	DATE:	Page 1 of 5

Form Ref: FC/F/DQP

ACTIVITY NO. (1)	ACTIVITY (2)	DEMANDING/CONTROLLING DOCUMENT (3)	VERIFICATION (4) CODE	BY	DATE	IDENTIFIED RECORD/VERIFYING DOCUMENT (5)	ISSUED TO (6) CODE	SIG	DATE
1	**Document Submissions**								
1.1	Detail quality plan	Spec. XYZ 623 FC/001	AH			Approved DQP	R		
1.2	Technical queries	CC 2093A FC/0013	A			TQ response	R		
1.3	Mould drawing and moulding procedure	CB/6372 CB/6373 CB/6374 FC/003 FC/0015	A			Approved drawing ABC/607 and procedure FC/0015	R		
1.4	Pre-and post-pour check sheets	FC/0018	A			Approved pre-and post-pour check sheets	R		
1.5	List of proposed manufacturers/sources of supply for: • cement • aggregates • admixes • reinforcement steel	FC/002 and FC/0011	A			Agreed list of sources of supply	R		
2	**Pre-manufacture**								
2.1	Issue contract document	FC/002 Agreed list of suppliers	I			Purchase orders Contracts	R		
2.2	Check material received to sampling plan	FC/0014 Purchase orders	P			Manufacturer's certificates	R		

Manufacture of Former Block 6 **QUALITY PLAN NO**: FCBC/62 **Page 2 of 5**

Form Ref: FC/F/DQP

Figure 7.5 Example front page and continuation sheets of a typical DQP (manufacturing phase) (Continued)

ACTIVITY NO. (1)	ACTIVITY (2)	DEMANDING/ CONTROLLING DOCUMENT (3)	VERIFICATION (4)			IDENTIFIED RECORD/VERIFYING DOCUMENT (5)	ISSUED TO (6)		
			CODE	BY	DATE		CODE	SIG	DATE
2.3	Check storage conditions	FC/006	Stores records				R		
2.4	Check calibration status of equipment	FC/005	Calibration records				R		
2.5	Prepare mould	FC/0015	I			Inspection certificate	R		
2.6	Prepare reinforcement		I				R		
2.7	Assembly mould around reinforcement		I				R		
3	**Pre-pour controls and inspections**	Pre-pour check sheet FC/0017							
3.1	Concrete batching		I			Batch certificate	R		
3.2	Concrete testing		I			Test certificate	R		
3.3	Permission to pour		I			Release note	R		
4	**Manufacture**								
4.1	Pour concrete		P			Inspection certificate	R		
4.2	Cure concrete		P				R		
4.3	Check results and identify test pieces		I				R		

Manufacture of Former Block 6   **QUALITY PLAN NO:** FCBC/62   **Page 3 of 5**

Form Ref: FC/F/DQP

ACTIVITY NO. (1)	ACTIVITY (2)	DEMANDING/ CONTROLLING DOCUMENT (3)	VERIFICATION (4)			IDENTIFIED RECORD/VERIFYING DOCUMENT (5)	ISSUED TO (6)		
			CODE	BY	DATE		CODE	SIG	DATE
5	**Post-pour checks**								
5.1	Strip mould	Post-pour check sheet FC/0019	F			Inspection certificate	R		
5.2	Lift and stack								
5.3	Identify								
5.4	Inspect								
6	**Rectifications**								
6.1	Repairs	FC/0018	I			Inspection certificate	R		
6.2	Concession applications	CC/2094B	A			Approved concession forms	R		
7	**Complete documentation**	FC/009	H, B			Client's release note	R, C		
Manufacture of Former Block 6						**QUALITY PLAN NO**: FCBC/62		**Page 4 of 5**	

Form Ref: FC/F/DQP

Figure 7.5 *Continued*

The following documents are referenced on the DQP and are shown here for information only.

Extracts from the Former Concrete Block Company Quality Manual:

Ref.	Procedure Title	Ref.	Procedure Title
FC/001	Preparation of quality plans	FC/0011	Control of suppliers
FC/002	Procurement of materials and services	FC/0012	Concessions
FC/003	Drawing preparation and approval	FC/0013	Technical queries
FC/004	Calculation preparation and approval	FC/0014	Goods receipt inspection
FC/005	Calibration	FC/0015	Mould preparation
FC/006	Stores control	FC/0016	Operation of batcher plant
FC/007	Preparation of inspection and test procedures	FC/0017	Preparation, curing and testing of concrete
FC/008	Pre- and post-pour checklists	FC/0018	Rectification of concrete blocks
FC/009	Documentation packages/records	FC/0019	Inspection of concrete blocks
FC/0010	Packing and dispatch		

Page 5 of 5

Figure 7.5 *Concluded*

Chapter 8

Choosing Support Services

Selection and evaluation criteria and techniques

When selecting and appointing others to carry out project activities, it is important that you can do so in the knowledge that they have both the competence and resources to successfully fulfil their assigned responsibilities. To bring this about requires two things:

Before you appoint suppliers you need to have confidence in their competence and resources.

1   You need to have a good understanding as to what is entailed with respect to the scope of work being placed – for example, its interface implications, time constraints, technical demands, resources and requisite management skills. Only if you have such understanding can you realistically hope to equate the needs of the work to the known capabilities of potential appointees.
2   You need to have up-to-date knowledge about the capabilities of those you are considering to appoint, preferably with this information expressed in a format which is easy to interpret and can be used with confidence.

This implies that you need a list of preferred suppliers which is updated on a regular basis to reflect the ongoing performances of those listed. So, what information do you need to have about an organization in order to decide whether it is suitable for inclusion on such a list?

*   **Financial stability**
    Does the organization have the financial assets and back-up needed to see a work programme through to completion? The implications of someone running out of funds part-way through a project extend far beyond the organization con-cerned, with typical 'knock-on' effects being:
    –   disruptions to the work programmes of others, with resulting claims
    –   project delays
    –   cost escalations
    –   adverse publicity
    –   client irritations.

    There may be many more.

*   **Technical suitability**
    What sort of business is the particular organization involved in? For example, is it an architectural practice, a design con-sultancy, a design and build contractor, a specialist contractor? In other words, what are the parameters of the services that can be offered?

*   **Resources**
    What scale of project work can the organization undertake? Are there limitations on the numbers of skilled personnel, equipment or back-up facilities that can be offered?

To what degree would external support be needed to cover functions not normally offered as part of the organization's mainstream capability?

- **Quality management capability**

  Does the organization operate a QMS which meets the requirements of a recognized standard such as ISO 9001:2000? If not, what does the organization have in place to address such issues as:
    - evaluating fully client requirements?
    - planning work programmes?
    - defining responsibilities?
    - organizing resources?
    - effectively carrying out planned activities?
    - checking, verification, validation activities?
    - monitoring ongoing process performance?
    - implementing prompt corrective actions if necessary?
    - collating records?

  If the organization does not have a QMS covering such tasks, you will need to learn how it selects and controls others if and when it delegates any part of its own work programme.

- **Health and safety**

  Because health and safety requirements are expressed in numerous regulations applicable to the construction industry, you need to be confident about the compliance process of any potential supplier or contractor.

- **Environmental factors**

  Although not all suppliers have yet fully grasped the implications of environmental legislation, the numbers that are now addressing this subject and seeking independent recognition of their system's performance against the relevant requirements of ISO 14001:1996 (Environmental Management System, specification with guidance for use) is increasing. It is worth noting that ISO 9001:2000, when drafted, was deliberately aligned with the ISO 14001 standard in order to enhance their capability for the benefit of the user community (see ISO 9001:2000, para. 0.4).

Having identified the sort of information you seek, what will guide you towards organizations which could be of interest?

The following are considered relevant, though not necessarily definitive:

- organizations known to you, which you have already used and which have consistently done a satisfactory job (in other words, those with a good track record)
- organizations recommended to you by sources you can trust

- organizations that you are asked to consider by your client(s)
- organizations which approach you directly, seeking consideration for their services, which fall within your scope of interest
- others – for example, organizations you may wish to consider because of their proximity to the project site.

In order to provide you with a detailed and comparable record of their capabilities, each organization (including those you have already used) should be asked to complete those parts of a standard questionnaire that are relevant to it.

Below is a typical example of relevant questions.

Example: Supplier Questionnaire

General

Name of organization: _____

Type of business engaged in: _____

Address: _____

Telephone, fax and e-mail numbers:_____

Number of years in business: _____

Number of permanent staff, with approximate breakdown by discipline: _____

_____

- Please give a short description of three projects recently undertaken, including names of clients and scopes of work.

_____

_____

- What are the value and nature of largest project(s) undertaken in the past two years? _____
- Please indicate any work-related limitations you may have – for example, regarding:
  - size of project
  - financial
  - geographic.

[Use separate sheet if necessary to elaborate.]

- Does the organization, when necessary, engage the support of, and manage, the activities of others?

YES/NO

- If the answer to the above is 'YES', how are the capabilities of such support organizations/persons determined as suitable prior to their appointment?
- Does the organization operate a 'preferred supplier list' or equivalent?

YES/NO

Quality Management

- Does the organization have a quality management system (QMS) compatible with the relevant requirements of ISO 9001:2000? YES/NO
- If the answer to the above is 'YES', has the system gained recognition from an accredited certification body? YES/NO
- If the answer to the above is 'YES', please provide the name of the certification body, date of certification and certificate number.
- If certification has not yet been applied for, is there any plan to do so in the foreseeable future? YES/NO
- If so when?
- Do you have a member of management who is responsible for the control and update of the QMS and/or the coordination of quality-related activities? YES/NO
- If so, please supply the person's name and position.
- Does the organization use quality plans in managing its project activities and/or request such plans from others working upon its behalf? YES/NO
- If your answer is 'YES' please provide an example of one of your typical plans.
- Do you have a quality manual? YES/NO
- If 'YES' will you please send:
  (a) an uncontrolled copy or
  (b) a copy of the index.
- Does the organization plan and implement a programme of internal audits? YES/NO
- If so, are these carried out by persons who have been trained in auditing technique? YES/NO

Health and Safety

- Does the organization have:
  (a) a health and safety policy? YES/NO
  (b) a health and safety officer? YES/NO
- Are all staff made fully aware of the various health and safety regulations which affect their work? For example:
  - the MHSW Regulations? YES/NO
  - the CDM Regulations? YES/NO
- Do staff receive formal training concerning health and safety matters? YES/NO
- Are there records of such training? YES/NO
- Has the organization ever provided the services of:
  (a) planning supervisor or
  (b) principal contractor
  as defined within the CDM Regulations 1994? If so, please give details.

- Does the organization carry out risk assessments?
  YES/NO
- If so, are measures resulting from such assessments effectively implemented, monitored and recorded?
  YES/NO
- Is the organization familiar with the purposes of:
  (a) health and safety plans?   YES/NO
  (b) a health and safety file?   YES/NO
- If you are a design organization, are you fully conversant with your responsibilities under Regulation 13 of the CDM Regulations 1994?   YES/NO
- Has the organization had any 'improvement notices' raised on it during the past five years?   YES/NO
- If 'YES', please give details.

Financial
- Please give the name of the organization's bankers.
- Does the organization produce an annual audited statement of its accounts?   YES/NO
  [If so, please provide a copy of most recent statement.]
- Please *provide details of any* professional indemnity insurance cover carried.

Environmental
- Does the organization have a declared environmental policy?   YES/NO
- Does the organization have an environmental management system compatible with the relevant expectations of ISO 14001:1996?   YES/NO
- If so, has such system received certification from an accredited certification body?   YES/NO
- In the absence of a formal environmental system, how does the organization recognize and give due consideration to environmental matters? [*For example, within risk assessments.*]
- Do staff receive training regarding the potential environmental impact of their work?   YES/NO
- If so, is such training recorded?   YES/NO

Note, however, that the questions within this questionnaire are merely indicative and not definitive. We would anticipate that your own organizations would need to include others, ideally within a standard 'questionnaire' document.

When seeking this information, make it clear that your purpose is to establish an up-to-date picture of the capabilities of the organization concerned so that you can more accurately match appropriate suppliers to the needs of specific projects.

Also, take care to stress that the information will be handled in the strictest confidence.

Preferred suppliers lists: use and control

Once you have gathered the information, it needs to be collated and expressed in a form which allows you to identify potentially suitable suppliers and compare their capabilities. This then essentially becomes your 'preferred supplier list'.

Many such lists include a rating system. For example:

Use a rating system in your preferred supplier list that allows you to speed up selecting a contractor, rather than slow the process down.

A would signify an organization which fully meets all the evaluation requirements and also had already successfully undertaken project work on your behalf.

B would signify *either* an organization which fully met all evaluation requirements, but had not yet completed a project assignment on your behalf *or* had essentially met all your requirements but had a known minor shortcoming needing to be addressed.

C would signify a supplier having known weaknesses and only to be considered as a last resort. Any bids received from such a supplier would need adjusting to compensate for actions/resources which you would have to take or provide in order to compensate for such deficiencies, probably rendering the bid non-competitive anyway.

Does the above mean that a supplier cannot possibly be considered unless they have an A or B rating? The answer is 'not necessarily'; there are exceptions.

For example, imagine that one of your suppliers is a small local family business which you have used for many years and which has never let you down, consistently producing results of a high standard, on time and at a competitive price. The work done has been of a generic nature. Are you going to debar such a supplier from doing further work on the grounds that it doesn't have a formal QMS? Hopefully not. What then do you need to do?

The answer is to ask the firm to produce a job-related DQP (see Chapter 7) on which will be identified:

- scope of work being undertaken
- key activities in sequence
- reference to any basic procedures, instructions or method statements used
- any inspection and measuring equipment or other special tools (for example, torque spanners) which would need to be calibrated before use
- inspections to be carried out
- health and safety measures

- responsibilities for carrying out activities and inspections
- records to be produced and their distributions.

Such a DQP would essentially be structured against your specified requirements (that is, a mini, job-specific, quality approach).

You would then need to pre-approve the plan as an adequate statement of intent, and your supplier would use it to control their work programme. A signed-off copy would then be submitted with the supplier's invoice so that you received evidence that all planned actions and verifications had taken place.

Occasionally a client may recommend a supplier you are not happy about and would not normally choose to use yourself. In such a case you must make your reservations known to the client and if you are then still asked to use the supplier, you should formally restate your reservations and any concerns about the consequences, as well as indicating the additional costs associated with the extra surveillance of the supplier required.

Obviously, as time goes by, your supplier records will grow. We recommend that you set up a file for each supplier, holding documents and information such as:

- initial questionnaire
- performance reports
- specimen quality plans
- correspondence

and so on.

Each file should be given a unique reference number, which will be included on your preferred suppliers list and thus enable quick access to the background to the various ratings.

Selecting potential suppliers

Once you have evaluated the demands of the work to be placed, you are in a position to consult your list and select a number of potential suppliers who can match the need.

Preference should be given to 'A'-rated organizations, because you know that they are adequate in all respects; this then allows you, in theory, to accept the lowest bid (after the usual response reviews).

If you have insufficient 'A'-rated organizations on your list (or if some are already overcommitted), you should move to 'B'-rated suppliers.

'C'-rated suppliers should only be used out of extreme necessity (for example, if you have no option other than to use a single-source supplier) and with caution.

The preferred suppliers list is a sensitive document and needs to be treated with an appropriate degree of confidentiality and with limited reader access only. If the information is stored on the computer, limited access restrictions should apply and the information should be 'read only', thus preventing sensitive information being left around the workplace or, even worse, finding its way outside the organization.

All of this indicates the need for good information control and, for this reason, we suggest that this should be part of the quality manager's responsibilities. The quality manager will thus:

- maintain the supplier files
- receive performance inputs
- amend the preferred list accordingly
- liaise as appropriate with the suppliers concerning the need for them to improve performance (this may have to be done through an intermediary – for example, the purchasing manager)
- provide advice to others on the relative strengths and weaknesses of potential appointees.

Figure 8.1 shows part of a typical preferred suppliers list.

The example list shown should extend and embrace other support organizations – for example:

- electrical contractors
- civil contractors
- mechanical contractors

and so on – depending on your regular support needs.

Because such a list will almost certainly be produced on a standard format and regularly updated, it will carry both a form number, page numbers and details of its issue status.

The generation, use and update of the list should be the subject of a QMS procedure.

Performance monitoring

To be of value, any list you have established needs to be updated and reflective of the actual performance of those you have used to carry out work on your behalf. Good performance will result in a retention, or even an upgrading, of a supplier's rating. Conversely, poor performance(s) will lead to downgrading or, in extreme cases, complete removal from your list, pending a time when failings can be shown to have been dealt with to your satisfaction.

Organization	Type of work carried out	Contact details	Performance rating	File ref no.
Straight & Line Ltd	Architects	6 Promenade Walk, Bromwell on Sea Lancs XV7 4DO	A	21
Muffle & Scuffle	Architects	'Bleak House' Crusty Lane Wallington WK1 2FL	A	22
Startem-Finishem and Partners	Architects	24 Cherry Walk Sunnington Bellow in Furnace BF6 9TL	A	23
Bloggs and Cogs Ltd	Architects	11 Tooth Lane Brassley Lancs XB6 6BX	B	24
Up-Down and Partners	Architects	4 Stairs Avenue Windley Cheshire CK7 4DY	B	25
Dawb & Dordle Ltd	Design Consultants	21 Plod Street Lockley Lancs SZ2 2PZ	A	31
Consteel Design Ltd	Design Consultants	10 Rockwell Gardens Poppington Cheshire CY3 3TL	B	34
Flunkit and Floggit Ltd	Design Consultants	6 Twopenny Lane Gadwell Staffs SW3 9ZX	A	36
PREFERRED SUPPLIERS LIST				
Form No: _____		Issue No: _____		
Date of Issue: _____		Page 1 of		

Figure 8.1 *Example of part of a hypothetical preferred suppliers list*

What, then, will be your main sources of performance-related information?

Typically these will be:

- feedback from such people as your client and the planning supervisor
- feedback from your own project staff on topics such as quality of workmanship, cooperation with others, attitudes, adequacy of resources
- the numbers of non-conformances recorded and rework required

Monitor a supplier's performance and use this to increase or decrease their rating in your list.

- corrective action reports
- audit findings.

Whatever the source of the input, it should not be just a matter of consequential feedback. You need to adopt a proactive approach to gathering key information using something like a simple questionnaire, to be completed at discrete stages of a work programme (for example, midway and on completion) so that comparative assessments can be made. Figure 8.2 shows a possible format for such a performance report. However, most organizations are likely to have their own formats for this purpose.

Finally, the suppliers questionnaire, the preferred suppliers list (showing the ratings) and the performance report form part of each supplier's file, which in turn will be part of the QMS records.

FINAL / INTERMEDIATE STAGE, PERFORMANCE REPORT
(Delete as appropriate)

Name of Organization: _____

Type of work carried out: _____

Project Ref.: _____

Site: _____

Report produced by: _____

(Signature please)

Position and date: _____

Points considered	Rating			Comments
	Excellent	Good	Poor	
Attitude/cooperation				
Standard of workmanship				
Work rate				
Health and safety awareness				
Delivery to programme and cost				
Document control and records				

Would you recommend re-use of this supplier on future projects?

Form No: _____

Figure 8.2 *Example supplier performance report*

Chapter 9

Applying the QMS to Project Work

Promoting bids and enhancing competitive edge

In Chapter 1 we spoke of the importance that a QMS can play in determining whether or not an organization will even be considered for undertaking project work by some clients.

If your client has stipulated that bidders must have and work in accordance with, a recognized QMS, you know immediately that you will be competing with other organizations that also have an established QMS. In these circumstances is there anything you can do that may just help to influence the client's decision in your favour? The answer is almost certainly 'yes'.

Put yourself in the position of your client who has stipulated that 'bidders' are required to have a QMS which satisfies those parts of ISO 9001:2000 relevant to 'the scope of work in question' and ask yourself which of the following two responses would convey the better impression.

- **Response 1**
  We confirm that the company has a quality management system which meets the relevant requirements of ISO 9001: 2000.

- **Response 2**
  We confirm that the company manages its activities in accordance with a formal quality management system structured to meet the relevant requirements of ISO 9001:2000.

  The system successfully gained third-party certification in 2001. We confirm that all project activities carried out on your behalf would be implemented in accordance with the above system which, if necessary, will be adapted to incorporate any specific requirements from yourselves.

  The company is also very conscious of its obligations to comply with prevailing health and safety regulations such as the CDM Regulations 1994 and the Management of Health and Safety at Work Regulations 1999, and the necessary provisions to ensure compliance with such regulations are integrated into the quality management system. In addition, the company monitors its quality management activities through a planned programme of internal audits and it would be our intention to ensure that this programme would positively monitor key activities on any project work undertaken on your behalf.

  Enclosed herewith is a copy of the index of our quality manual from which you will be able to readily appreciate the scope of our system.

> Make use of your QMS to win business – tell clients how you address quality and service on their behalf.

Should you require any further information on this subject, please do not hesitate to contact our quality manager, _____, Tel. no._____.

When competing with other organizations that also have a QMS the extra few words can make a significant difference, even if only to plant ideas in the client's mind such as: 'I wonder what the others do about health and safety and positive monitoring?'.

If you have, and can offer, something of value to your client, say so. If you don't, others may.

If you are bidding in a situation where formal quality management has not been stipulated, our advice is to promote your capability nevertheless. It may be that the client is not fully aware of the benefits of the quality management approach, but your submission may well generate thoughts such as: 'This is of interest. I wonder what the others do to manage their work programme.' The answer might be 'Not a lot'.

When you carry out the initial review of your client's requirements, try to read between the lines. Why is a QMS requirement being made? Almost certainly it is because your client feels that, if you have a QMS, the work can be delegated with confidence in the knowledge that things will (or should be) properly managed. Why not reinforce that confidence with those few extra words?

What you emphasize may vary from project to project. For example, you may wish to stress that all activities will be carried out in accordance with a project-specific quality plan and then submit a typical specimen of such a plan, highlighting how key interfaces with the client, such as joint meetings, stage approvals and document submissions, are recognized, just to demonstrate an appreciation of your client's input and participation.

Think about how to explain your QMS capability in your brochures or marketing literature.

We also recommend that serious thought be given to the ways in which your QMS capability can be projected not only in bid documentation, but also in publicity brochures and literature describing the reasons why people should choose *your* services.

Why merely display a certification logo on the bottom of the back page of such promotional material when it is the significance of the logo in terms of customer benefit that needs to be projected? *Do not sell your organization short.*

The design office

We have already emphasized how the design function is fundamental to project success. It is at this stage that such things as:

- selections of materials
- levels of stress

- safety factors
- structural configurations
- handling, fabrication and erection requirements
- bills of materials
- specifications/instructions to others

and so on are established.

The importance of the design stage cannot be over-emphasized. Everything that follows this stage is about meeting the design requirements. If a design is flawed, the subsequent meeting of its requirements will merely produce weakness, failure or even disaster. There is no stage in the construction cycle where the need for the application of sound, visible control disciplines is more evident. This is why the QMS is so significant.

Of particular importance during the design phase are the PQP and design reviews.

The project quality plan

The PQP is the key document for managing project activities. Whereas your QMS will contain procedures concerning many design activities, such as preparing calculations, drawings, verifications, structure of a project file, risk assessments, document controls and so on, it is the PQP which equates the QMS to the specific needs of the project. It identifies, amongst other things:

- the project brief
- the project team (that is, the right, trained people)
- applicable standards, regulations and so on
- applicable procedures
- work programmes
- liaison and communication links and routes
- records.

This document, in essence, defines, through its various referenced items of information, what is to be done, by whom, how and in what sequence.

In short, the PQP, and adherence to its requirements, is the key to design stage success.

Design reviews

Design reviews are a second key to success. Technical by nature, attended by knowledgeable people, representative of the activities being carried out and held at appropriate stages in the evolution of the design, these reviews check and confirm that those things essential to design success have happened. The following are typical of the sorts of questions that may be asked at various stages of the design process.

Assumptions are dangerous. Always check that important stages of the design process have been completed satisfactorily.

Initial stage

- Has all necessary information been received from the client?
- Are all necessary design base standards, regulations and so on identified and available?
- Has the project file been opened?
- Has the PQP been established?
- Has an initial meeting been held with the planning supervisor?
- Has the client been made aware of their responsibilities under the CDM regulations?
- Are we able to start our design activities?

Intermediate stage

- Are all activities proceeding to plan?
- Have all key calculations been produced and verified, and do they confirm the design integrity?
- Has a risk assessment been carried out?
- Has the design been amended to eliminate risk situations?
- Where such elimination has not been possible or considered practicable, has the planning supervisor been advised?
- Are all pre-identified support facilities (for example, computer services) being made available?
- Have all due notifications to others been made in a timely manner?
- Have the minutes of all key meetings been circulated to the necessary people?
- Is the project file up-to-date?
- Are there any anticipated problems needing attention?

End of project

- Have all drawings been approved and issued?
- Have all planned activities been completed?
- Have all required information distributions been made?
- Is/are the project file/records complete and up-to-date?
- Have any problems been encountered which require further consideration in order to prevent their future recurrence?
- Has client comment on our project performance been sought?
- Was the client satisfied?
- If not, what have we done/can we do to improve future performance?
- Has the client been thanked and informed accordingly?

The construction contractor

There are a number of different types of contract arrangements – for example:

- **Turnkey**
  Here, the client appoints a single organization to be responsible for the design and construction management of the whole project. If the contractor does not provide the design services direct, the usual approach will be to form a consortium or enter into partnership with a suitable design organization.

- **Construction management**
  Here the appointed contractor liaises directly with the client and assumes responsibility for the management and construction activities, excluding design.

- **Independent contractors**
  Here the contractor(s) do not work directly for the client/owner. Instead they report to an intermediary such as the resident engineer, architect or consultant.

Regardless of which arrangement prevails, the key responsibilities of the contractor do not differ greatly.

The example below shows a list of typical contractor activities in sequential order, with associated notes describing how various aspects of the QMS addressed in this book relate to the activities in question.

Example: List of Typical Contractor Activities

1 Receive enquiry and acknowledge (document control procedure).

2 Review information (note any specific conditions concerning quality management, health and safety, CDM Regulations and so on) and ensure that you can resource the work programme within the specified time objectives.

   Resolve any unclear aspects of information received or request additional information if something that you feel is significant is not included. Confirm formally (contract review procedure).

3 Submit a well-presented and qualified bid (tendering procedure).

4 On receipt of the contract (assumed), again review details to ensure that no changes have been made to the information/requirements which were tendered against. If any changes have been

---

introduced, resolve any implications and confirm formally (contract review procedure).

5   Establish the contract team (management responsibility).

6   Prepare the quality plan(s) (see Chapter 7 on the preparation and use of quality plans).

7   Identify suitable contractors (suppliers) for the provision of any required support services, based on their known capability and resources. (Use the preferred suppliers list – see Chapter 8).

8   Invite those identified at (7) above to bid for work, ensuring that bid invitation specifications include all relevant requirements to be met including those for quality management and health and safety (tender invitation procedure).

9   Appoint support contractors, subject to any third-party approval (such as the client), when necessary.

10 Control off-site contractors (if any). This may be achieved through a variety of measures which should have been defined at the invitation to tender stage.

    One ideal way of enabling this is through the preparation, by the appointed contractor, of a DQP identifying in sequence all the key activities to be carried out, the demanding document(s) (for example, specification, standard, procedure) against which each would be implemented, levels of verification, records, distributions of information and so on. This would then be submitted to you prior to the commencement of work, for your approval and the incorporation of any additional requirements you felt necessary. (See Chapter 7 on DQPs.)

11 Control work on site. In addition to the usual inspections, site meetings and so forth, the preparation and submission of a DQP by support contractors can again prove very useful, incorporating steps to be followed by each in carrying out their various work programmes and, also including as appropriate, health and safety measures such as:

    • reviewing health and safety plan requirements.
    • liaising with the principal contractor concerning such matters as:-
        – risk assessments
        – health surveillance
        – mutually shared equipment
        – harmonizing work programmes.

Whether you are acting as principal contractor or as an intermediary between the principal contractor and those engaged to support you, it is essential that arrangements for health and safety are made known to everyone (see Chapter 6).

Throughout the site construction phase all activities will be carried out in accordance with the stipulated (and monitored) requirements of your own quality plan (step 6 above) until all activities are seen to have been completed, desired outcomes have been achieved and appropriate records generated.

12 Collate and present records. If your contract quality plan and the various DQPs, prepared by your support contractor and approved by you, have been properly implemented, all the necessary records needed for incorporation in the health and safety file, including those for the client, for yourself, your support contractors and any others, will have been identified, progressively produced and correctly distributed to the right persons and destinations (for example, to contract files) and evidence of this will be apparent by virtue of:

- annotation of the plans themselves, confirming that distributions were made
- relevant cover notes/letters
- formal acknowledgements of receipt
- check of the appropriate contract files.

All the above, along with other documents, from invitation to tender to handover acceptance, will then form the total contract records.

Chapter **10**

Monitoring Business/ Process Effectiveness

Business performance

In this chapter we look at some of the techniques you can use to monitor and improve your business performance.

You need to constantly seek to improve your performance and, to do this, you need to know:

- how well you are performing now
- where there is scope for improvement
- what you need to do in order to improve
- how effective any measures you have taken have been

and then continue to repeat this process.

Merely taking a reactive approach to making improvements – that is, waiting until something is obviously wrong and then fixing it – is not enough. You need to adopt a proactive approach, which means continually reviewing your business and process performances to see whether there is any scope for improvement.

Pressure of work may sometimes make it difficult to find the time to take an objective view of the way you do things. We have all heard the saying, 'If it works, why change it?'.

There's no advantage in change for change's sake. On the other hand, is everything you do necessary or could some things be done better?

However, we are not suggesting change for change's sake. We are saying that the fact that something works does not mean that it is still necessary or cannot be further improved.

Improvements cannot be made without knowing how well you are currently doing things. Only this knowledge allows you to assess the potential benefits of any proposed improvements, preferably in measurable terms in order to quantify its benefit and guide any decision to improve it.

Any improvements you make should align with the policies and declared objectives of your business, one of which will certainly be achieving and maintaining customer satisfaction. Although it is tempting to read this as meaning the external customer, namely your client, who commissions your services and pays you, hopefully for a job well done, you must not lose sight of your internal customers – namely, your downstream customers who rely upon the quality of your output to provide their required input.

Customer satisfaction and techniques for identifying scopes for improvement

Face-to-face discussion

Don't just assume you are doing a good job – find out!

Your first step should be to ask your external and internal customers whether they are satisfied with your performance and the services you have provided. This may sound obvious and fundamental, but it is surprising how many organizations assume that because they receive no complaints and are paid (in the case of the external customer) everything is/was perfectly satisfactory.

It is dangerous to make such assumptions – why not ask a few simple questions face-to-face?

Ask the external customer:

- Are you satisfied with the services we have provided?
- Is there anything you feel we could have done/could do better?
- If so, how would it have helped you?
- Would you recommend us to others?
- Would you use us again?

Ask the internal customer:

- Was/is the service/information provided right for your needs?
- What, if anything, can we do better to provide what you need?
- What are your key needs – that is, those things, that are essential to enable you to do your job?

Obviously there are many other ways of gathering information, but direct discussion with a person of suitable position and authority is, we believe, the best method because it enables you to develop the subjects discussed.

Questionnaires

Another form of gathering information is through the use of well-structured questionnaires, asking questions of the type raised above. However, the weaknesses of this approach are as follows:

- You can get very closed (yes/no) answers to certain questions when you really need to establish the 'because' element.
- Sometimes questionnaires can be looked upon as 'junk mail' and either ignored or delegated to a subordinate for completion.
- If you wish to seek elaboration of a response, it can prove irritating for the customer and hence counterproductive for you.

The secrets of making questionnaires effective are as follows:

- Direct them to a specific person, as a confidential request.
- Explain why you need the information – for example:
  - because you value and want your customer's constructive input
  - because it is your organization's policy to continuously improve your processes.
- Make it convenient to respond by enclosing a prepaid return envelope.
- Never forget to thank people formally for their time and effort in responding.

Using key performance indicators (KPIs)

In essence, this is an approach for identifying indicators that can tell you whether your organization and its processes are effectively delivering the results you are aiming for, or where scope for improvement exists. The information gathered gives an indication of how well your company is performing against agreed standards.

The following important points should be kept in mind when using this approach:

- Top management should be involved in selecting appropriate indicators.
- They should relate to the business policy objectives.
- They must be measurable and measured at suitable intervals in order to produce meaningful data.
- Choosing a few important KPIs with reference to business performance is more effective than having too many.

Choosing subjects for KPIs

For your *external* customers the KPIs should be based on the customer's known expectancies and should have a real impact on your business performance – for example:

KPIs should focus on those things that are key to continuing good customer relationships.

- the submission of specific documents, such as drawings for approval within a specified timescale.
- qualified responses to technical queries within a specified period.

In other words, you should base your KPIs on those things on which your continuing good relationships with your external customer depend.

For your *internal* customers your KPIs should be based on the things that affect your business performance (perhaps relating to the balance sheet) – for example:

- absenteeism figures
- closing out of audits findings within an agreed timescale
- the number of accidents in the workplace
- process owners responding to requests to alter the process within a given timescale
- issuing of invoices within so many days of handover.

Whatever specific KPIs you choose, they need to be defined, measured in an agreed manner at predetermined intervals by designated staff and their findings presented in an agreed format.

Each KPI should have a nominated owner who will collect the data, process it and report to top management. In turn, top management should review the KPI reports at set frequencies and take the appropriate action – for example:

- If performance gradually improves, pass this positive information back to staff.
- If performance deteriorates, consider modifying the process or taking any other appropriate action to address the problem.
- Modify the KPI if it is not providing useful data.

Team meetings

Team meetings, where you can invite input from attendees concerning possible improvements to the various business processes, can be a further source of improvement information. These inputs can be reviewed by the attendees for further consideration and action.

In-built provision within the QMS

Any good QMS will include the mechanisms for any system user, at any time, to submit qualified suggestions for improvement through specific channels. See Chapter 3.

Audits

The subject of auditing is too big to adequately cover within this particular book, so the following is merely a short outline concerning this particular review and information-gathering technique.

The quality management audit

There are many kinds of audit – financial and stocktaking to cite just two examples. The kind that we are highlighting here, however, is known as a quality management audit because it is concerned with the way in which tasks and processes are done and managed, particularly those relating to the achievement of quality.

An audit is a management tool for the independent assessment of any process or activity and, in reality, a quality management audit is an examination to determine the adequacy, availability and understanding of and/or the adherence to a process, system or programme.

Subjects for consideration by internal audits include:

- the effectiveness of the strategy, objectives and policies
- the effectiveness and efficiency of processes
- customer interfaces
- the effectiveness of performance measures
- the analysis of quality costs.

Audits are usually conducted against specific requirements, such as a relevant quality standard (for example, ISO 9001:2000) or, more usually, the organization's own QMS.

The importance of audits

There are many reasons why audits are both necessary and important. First, it is important to know that any system being operated remains relevant to, and adequate for, the needs of the business. Things change. Technology changes. You need to create and maintain your competitive edge. This means that systems pointing the way to the achievement of quality objectives must be dynamic and subject to ongoing review and change if necessary. *The audit is a review technique.*

Second, the system is only a means to an end; it is not an end in itself. What is important is that those performing tasks are correctly adhering to the system. The audit checks and confirms (or otherwise) this situation and, where necessary, indicates corrective actions.

Third, audits tend to keep people on their toes and underline the need for continuous commitment to the laid-down system.

Types of audit

Basically, the organization might be involved in three types of audit, namely:

- *External audits*
  These are independent audits carried out by one organization (or on its behalf) on the system of another organization.

- *Self-audits*
  These are normally carried out by management on its own processes and do not follow the traditional audit approach. They are sometimes referred to as 'improvement audits' and are described at the end of this section.

- *Internal audits*
  These are independent audits carried out by an organization on its own internal systems or working practices.

Of these types, we are essentially concerned with the internal audit, as the findings can contribute to business improvements.

Internal audits

The internal audits planned to be carried out in your company will generally be process, project/contract or system-related.

- **Process audits**

  The emphasis in ISO 9001:2000 is on the 'process approach'. Such audits will look at the transformation of inputs into outputs, often the output of one process becoming the input to the next. The process audit will therefore look closely at the control at interfaces and the transmission of information within the organization.

  Process audits can be carried out at any time and may examine such things as:
    - control of work processes
    - the purchasing process
    - the records management process.

- **Contract/project audits**

  Such audits will usually examine the specific quality programme pertaining to a particular package of work. They are usually carried out at discrete stages in the work programme – for example, design, procurement, fabrication, erection, test and so on.

- **System audits**

  System audits examine the organization's quality system. They will cover all, or a selection of, departments engaged in carrying out quality-related activities/ processes and examine their organization and systems of control. Such audits may be internal – that is, examining your own system and adherence to it by those performing tasks – or 'external' – that is, examining suppliers' systems.

The internal audit sequence

1 Prepare and issue audit schedule, annually.
2 Appoint a team leader.
3 Hold a pre-audit meeting.
4 Select audit team.
5 Obtain and review documentation related to the scope of the audit.
6 Prepare checklists. Base these checklists on the requirements of ISO 9001:2000, which state that more emphasis should now be placed on the company's policies and business objectives. This means checking people's understanding of responsibilities, ownership of processes, effectiveness of processes, continuous improvement policy, satisfying the client and so on.
7 Prepare and issue the audit programme.
8 Hold the opening meeting.
9 Conduct the audit, ask questions, examine evidence and record non-compliances and observations.
10 Verbally agree the non-compliances.
11 Collate the findings.
12 Report the findings (both good and bad) at the closing meeting.

13 Agree a corrective action programme (CAP) or possible improvements.
14 Prepare and issue an audit report.
15 Monitor the CAP and close out the audit.
16 Compile records.

Feedback from internal audits

Audits are only of value if
their findings are properly
responded to.

It is a waste of time carrying out internal audits if the findings are
not used to improve the business processes. In the past, many
organizations have carried out internal audits because it is a
requirement of ISO 9001:2000 clause 8.2.2 without obtaining the
full potential from the auditing process.

Real benefits can be obtained from the auditing process if you
do it properly, but to obtain genuine improvements to your
management system you need to do the following:

- Use trained auditors.
- Ensure that there is commitment from top management to
  provide the resources to carry out the audit programme and to
  raise corrective actions to be completed in a timely manner.
- Ensure that feedback on the effectiveness of audits, resulting
  from any corrective actions taken, are fed into the management
  review process.

Self-audits

Together with internal audits, top management should also consider
implementing a self-audit programme. Although not a mandatory
requirement of ISO 9001:2000, a number of organizations have
practised self-audits with great success as a useful tool for improve-
ing the QMS and business performance.

As distinct from 'internal audits' which are independent activities,
'self-audits' are carried out by the organization's own management.
It involves monitoring the small number of important factors on
which the success of a process or project hinges. The 'process
owner' or project manager then carries out personal spot checks
(self-audits) to ensure that these key activities have taken or are
taking place in a proper or timely manner, thus providing a degree
of confidence in achieving a successful process or project result.

Subjects to be considered for self-audits could be:

- *Design office*: close-out of actions from design review
  meetings, risk assessments being available for the planning
  supervisor and so on.
- *Construction project*: availability of as-built drawings, follow-
  up and response to customer complaints and so on.

The self-audit technique is a good one, for several reasons:

- It is simple to understand because the auditors (management staff within a department or area of work), are only reviewing the processes that they themselves manage on a daily basis.
- It demands management commitment to the process. Managers have to be involved in deciding the scope of the audits and therefore can choose the subject matter, which will lead to improvements within their department.
- Self-audits are easy to carry out because they are normally of a short duration (say, one to two hours), are carried out in a localized work area and generally have a limited scope.
- Because self-audits take a short time to carry out and report, there is a limited impact on resources.
- Because managers are auditing their own processes, they are more likely to pick up problems than an internal auditor, who may only visit that work area, to audit, once a year.
- Self-audits tend to focus employees' attention and keep them on their toes.
- Managers only need a small amount of training to carry out self-audits and carrying them out gives them a good understanding of where the real problems lie.

When planning self-audits in your organization you should consider the following points:

- Don't initially apply self-audits right across the organization, especially if they have never been employed previously. Try them out in selected areas on one part of the QMS and extend their range when benefits can be demonstrated.
- Choose areas for which the audit feedback will help you, as a manager, improve the performance of your department or team.
- Feed the results of the self-audits into the management review process.

The management review

Management reviews are periodic (for example, annual or bi-annual) meetings held by senior management to review the continuing adequacy of the organization's policies, objectives, strategy and processes in relation to changing market expectations, past performance and so forth. Its aim is to identify where there may be scope for improvements that will lead to:

- enhanced reputation and market share
- greater competitiveness
- improved performance and business results.

The range of subjects discussed will relate to factors that are both internal and external to the organization, and the findings dictate significant matters such as forward strategy and business plans.

Normally, such reviews will be chaired by a senior executive, such as the managing director, and attended by the other directors/process owners. One attendee will (or should) be the quality manager, who may not attend full-time, but will be expected to report upon such matters as the effectiveness of the QMS, results of audits, corrective and preventive action needed and taken, indications for system/process improvements, degree of customer satisfaction and so on.

Set out below is an indicative (though not definitive) list of subjects which may be included in the agenda for a management review meeting:

- Market research findings
- Results of benchmarking initiatives
- Competitor information
- Feedback on KPIs
- Customer satisfaction data
- Organization policies and business strategy
- Highlights, improvements in the QMS and its overall effective-ness
- Audit findings (including any self-audits) and the status of corrective and preventive actions
- Process performances and adequacies
- Changes to previous assumptions (for example, as a result of new regulations, financial, social or environmental factors)
- New/emerging technologies, quality concepts and so on
- Status and effectiveness of agreed actions resulting from previous review
- Possible joint initiatives with others
- Improved/additional resource needs.

Some organizations may favour adopting a two-stage manage-ment review procedure, whereby the key process owners review events within their scopes of responsibility, prior to collating their findings and proposals at a second top-tier review with all the senior personnel present.

Improvement initiatives

Throughout this book (and within this chapter) there has been frequent mention of:

- processes and their ownership
- setting measurable improvement objectives
- collecting performance data as an indicator of potential further improvements.

There are, however, other measures, which are proactive as opposed to reactive, and which can be taken towards process improvement, provided that top management is supportive.

The following technique is taken from one of the courses within a five-course business improvement series that has been run by one of the authors of this book for several years. The technique:

- focuses on the customer
- is proactive (that is, it does not merely react to identified problem situations)
- harnesses the strength of teamworking and, as such, offers the many benefits that we described in Chapter 1.
- involves all levels of staff and increases their interest and commitment
- expresses outputs in measurable terms
- is not difficult to apply and would ideally only be applied once or twice in any year
- is successful because its results are based on the collective and coordinated inputs of selected staff who are knowledgeable about the process under review, working together on a team basis.

The methodology

The following describes the steps involved.

Prioritizing processes

You need to establish which are your key processes and why.

Although all processes are important, some are more important than others because they directly interface with the external customer/client or affect everyone within the organization, as opposed to just a few. Other processes may be considered important because of their financial implications. Whatever the criteria decided by top management, the first step is to attempt to prioritize the company's various processes.

One useful way of doing this is to use a simple chart such as that shown in Figure 10.1. The idea is to rate the answer to each question in terms of its significance, using a scale of 1–10.

For example, if you considered 'internal auditing' as the process to be assessed, you would record a nil rating for question 1, high ratings for questions 2, 3 and 5 and medium ratings for questions 4 and 6, indicating that auditing is an important process with a significant impact on total business performance. Your total score would probably be something like 40 out of 60. Obviously you would adapt this chart to suit your own processes in terms of both type and number of questions.

PROCESS PRIORITIZATION FORM

CONSIDERATIONS

PROCESS AND RELATED PROCEDURES	1 Does the process interface directly with external customers?	2 Does the process affect *all* work areas or staff?	3 Does the process affect multiple work areas and staff?	4 Does the process entail health and safety or environmental issues?	5 Does the process have a major influence on business performance?	6 Does the process represent a significant % of total expenditure?	Total

Form no: ....

(Rank from 1–10)

1 (insignificant) ◄──────► 10 (significant)

Issue: ....

Figure 10.1 *Process prioritization form*

Selecting a process for evaluation

The process to be evaluated will normally be selected through management review.

The reasons for selection would typically be:

- the significance of the process
- the length of time since the methodology has been looked at
- evidence of problem indicators.

Overall monitoring and support

Once the decision to conduct a process improvement initiative has been taken, a small management steering committee should be formed. This should be made up of two or more senior management personnel who have a good understanding of the process and the relevant procedures plus an appreciation of process cost data and failure costs.

Details of the selected process, customer (for example, client or recipient of the process output) and process end-product (objective) as seen by the organization should be entered by the secretary of the steering committee into Part 1 of a form similar to that shown in Figure 10.2.

The steering committee then agrees the objectives and strategy of the initiative. Typically, this would be:

- **Objective**: to improve the current process and qualify/quantify improvements in measurable terms.

- **Strategy**: to analyse the present situation and, in cooperation with, and considering the inputs of, staff who are knowledgeable about the process, identify, agree and qualify/ quantify any proposed changes along with the criteria for measuring their value-adding effectiveness.

A target timescale for carrying out the initiative up to the point of submitting a 'proposal report' is then established.

Appointing and briefing a team leader

The next step is for the steering committee to appoint a team leader to lead the practical aspects of the initiative. The person chosen will ideally:

- have a good understanding of the process and its integral activities
- be able to demonstrate an open, fair-minded attitude to others
- be acceptable to others

- be a good communicator and listener
- have good coordinating skills
- be able to encourage others to participate fully
- enjoy challenge and have a genuine enthusiasm for the task.

The team leader is then briefed on the initiative, the selected process, the parameters to be covered, and the objectives and strategy to be deployed.

Confirming the initiative team

The next step is to choose team members representing different levels of staff – ideally, those who have 'hands-on' process knowledge, and will therefore be able to make a valid contribution. Team members can include people from customer groups in those cases where the process output is internal to the organization (for example, the auditee in the case of the internal audit process).

Confirming customer (internal or external) expectations

The team leader should now make direct contact with a selection of customers (internal and external) to determine what their expectations are, and what they regard as particularly important and why.

The findings from these discussions are formally recorded, using Part 2 of the form illustrated in Figure 10.2. One form is used for each customer.

The team leader is now in a position to compare the expectations of the organization's customers with the previously recorded expectations. Any differences are noted down using Part 3 of the form. From this information the team leader can now prepare an action plan identifying the customer requirements that each process should aim to meet as a minimum.

A copy of the specification should then be sent to the steering committee.

Briefing the team

Next, the team leader holds an initial meeting with the team in order to:

- define the purpose of the exercise
- explain the objectives and implementation strategy
- describe the actions taken to date and the findings recorded as a result of the meetings with the customers.

CUSTOMER REQUIREMENTS INFORMATION	
Process description:	
Customer/recipient of process output:	
Type of product/service normally to be provided:	**Part 1**
Type of product/service needed/preferred by customer plus supporting comments (e.g. problems/weaknesses):	**Part 2**
Main differences between Part 1 and Part 2, e.g. speed, information, formats/breakdowns etc.	**Part 3**
Other comments:	
Date of discussion: **Participants:** **Signed:** .... **Team Leader**	
Form no: .... **Issue**	

Figure 10.2 *Customer requirements information*

Establishing the 'as-is' situation

Following the team briefing the team collectively prepare and agree a flowchart of the current process, identifying all process steps, inputs, outputs and interfaces with other processes.

This first meeting concludes with each team member being given a copy of the current flowchart together with the action plan previously produced by the team leader.

A provisional date for the next meeting is set, prior to which all the team members are required to study the information given to them and to draft their thoughts about improvements to the current process. To assist individual thinking during this review stage, a guideline checklist, along the lines of the example below, is also distributed.

Example: Checklist for Reviewing Process Steps

Can we:

- Eliminate any of the process steps/activities, in total or in part, without jeopardizing the process itself? YES/NO

  If yes:
  How?
  By how much?
  To what benefit?
  At what cost?

- Combine steps/activities to better effect? YES/NO

  If yes:
  How?
  By how much?
  To what benefit?
  At what cost?

- Reduce staffing levels (number/grade)? YES/NO

  If yes:
  How?
  By how much?
  To what benefit?
  At what cost?

- Reduce process times? YES/NO

  If yes:
  How?
  By how much?
  To what benefit?
  At what cost?

- Use better technology? YES/NO

  If yes:
    How?
    By how much?
    To what benefit?
    At what cost?

- Reduce errors, stoppages and wastage? YES/NO

  If yes:
    How?
    By how much?
    To what benefit?
    At what cost?

- Eliminate or reduce problems and
  needs for corrective action? YES/NO

  If yes:
    How?
    By how much?
    To what benefit?
    At what cost?

- Express things in a simpler way? YES/NO

  If yes:
    How?
    By how much?
    To what benefit?
    At what cost?

- Reduce or increase external support
  for the improvement of the process? YES/NO

  If yes:
    How?
    By how much?
    To what benefit?
    At what cost?

- Stimulate or specify requirements more
  clearly and in a more timely manner? YES/NO

  If yes:
    How?
    By how much?
    To what benefit?
    At what cost?

- Improve environmental conditions? YES/NO

  If yes:
    How?
    By how much?
    To what benefit?
    At what cost?

- Improve health and safety aspects?　　　YES/NO

  If yes:
  How?
  By how much?
  To what benefit?
  At what cost?

- Improve people's understanding,
  commitment and job satisfaction?　　　YES/NO

  If yes:
  How?
  By how much?
  To what benefit?
  At what cost?

After the meeting, the minutes should be produced and agreed before being distributed to both the attendees and the steering committee.

Individual reviews

Each team member should now review the current process flowchart in the light of the latest customer needs/expectations and any shortcomings that may have been identified. The checklist set out above should be used as an *aide-mémoir*, the object being to structure an improved process.

Where problems have been identified with the current process, thoughts concerning their probable root causes and appropriate remedial actions should be recorded.

Evaluating process effectiveness

At the second meeting of the team (more than one meeting may be required for this critical stage), the individual inputs from each member are discussed, compared, developed, accepted or discounted by mutual agreement. Information concerning identified problems should, if deemed necessary, be analysed in depth using tools such as cause and effect diagrams, so that all possible root causes can be identified and considered.

The checklist should be used again, and each step of any proposed revised process questioned concerning its necessity, sequence, real benefit and so on. The objective of the meeting is to draft a revised process which the team consider fully takes account of the latest known needs of both the customer and the organization as a whole, expressed in the most effective way.

Minutes of the meeting should then be distributed as previously.

Reviewing process efficiency

Although this may be done in parallel with the evaluation described above, it will more usually be done as a 'follow-up' team exercise.

Having decided at the previous stage what will be an 'effective' process (for example, doing the right things), the team now need to consider the most 'efficient' way each step can or should be implemented. At this stage, matters such as available technology, levels of responsibility required and use of new or revised documentation are discussed and agreed.

Again, minutes should be prepared and distributed as before.

Quantifying and qualifying predicted benefits and implementation costs and resources

The team should now review the proposed process revisions and the predicted tangible benefits such as less activities, reduced activity times, costs and staffing levels, which should be listed and quantified in measurable terms. Similarly foreseeable intangible benefits, such as improved customer satisfaction, better staff awareness/understanding, improved working environment and so on, should also be listed.

Anticipated times, resources and costs considered necessary to implement any proposed changes should now also be estimated. These may typically include possible limited staff retraining, revisions to the documented QMS among other things. During this stage input from others – for example, the cost accountant – may be sought to help ensure the accuracy of any forecasts made.

Reporting the conclusions

Next, a formal report should be prepared by the team leader and submitted to the steering committee. This should include:

- a brief description of the selected process
- objectives of the review
- the strategy followed
- the names of persons involved – that is:
    - steering committee members
    - team leader
    - team members
    - contacts
    - others
- an overall summary and recommendations
- predicted tangible benefits
- predicted intangible benefits
- estimation of implementation resources, costs and timescale
- a flowchart illustrating the proposed revised process.

Deciding on actions

The report should now be considered by the steering committee and further qualified at their request if necessary. It then needs to be raised at the next board of directors meeting and a decision made regarding implementation or otherwise. If the proposals are accepted, the team should prepare and implement an action plan.

Post-implementation monitoring

When you monitor progress can be as important as *how* you monitor it.

Progress should be monitored at an appropriate time – in other words, at a time when the anticipated improvements given in the formal report are taking effect.

A good way of doing this is by means of an improvement audit using staff trained in auditing techniques, but addressing specific aspects only. Questions that might be considered include:

- Was the agreed implementation plan followed completely and in a timely manner?
- How did the implementation costs compare with those forceast?
- Have the anticipated tangible benefits been realized?
- Has the revised process led to improved customer satisfaction?
- What evidence is there of this?
- What lessons (if any) have been learned for future improvement initiatives?
- Has the QMS been properly updated?

The audit report should be prepared and distributed on limited circulation only, through the quality manager.

Final note

In some organizations, the cost of carrying out the improvement initiative may be offset against the anticipated short-term financial benefits of any proposed improvements. In others, it will be absorbed under a general overhead provision. It is all a matter of organizational policy.

The benefits of such initiatives can be very significant indeed – for example, an annual bottom-line saving of £25 000 may well equate to ten times that amount in terms of sales revenue.

Auditing success

Auditing success is a targeted approach to monitoring improvements achieved. We have already described in the previous section how the technique can be applied to measuring the effectiveness of improvement initiatives, but it is equally applicable to any other activity for which measurable improvement objectives have been established. An example might be monitoring whether the information resulting from KPIs has been properly collected, collated, acted upon and to what effect.

Auditing success provides an independent overview and produces valuable feedback on the effectiveness of the approaches being examined.

Updating the QMS

As shown in Figure 1.1 your QMS is a dynamic reflection of your current best working practices. More importantly, it is the key vehicle for conveying to everyone within the organization the need to continually and collectively seek to satisfy their customers by doing the things they do as effectively and efficiently as possible.

To this end, it is important that everyone within the organization has a sense of ownership for the system and feels that it reflects what they do in a manner with which they can fully identify, and also that any opportunities they see for making system improvements will be welcomed.

In this chapter we have described a number of tools for system review and improvement update – for example, internal audits, setting and monitoring performance indicators, improvement initiatives, auditing improvements and management reviews. However, these tools are only of value if properly used and their results fed back and reflected in a continuing improvement of the QMS itself.

Those who grasp wholeheartedly the 'quest for improvement' nettle will find it will lead not only to better business performance, but also to a competitive edge over their competitors. Can you afford to stand still?

Chapter **11**

Recognition of the QMS

After spending considerable time and effort you now have a QMS in place. Following a trial introductory period to iron out any teething problems, it has been issued, company-wide, to all staff.

Following the introduction of the QMS you introduced a programme of internal audits (first-party audits) to confirm that:

- it was an accurate interpretation of the company processes
- it met the requirements of the quality standard ISO 9001:2000
- staff were working to procedures and processes as identified in the QMS.

You have now operated the QMS for a period of time (say, 6–12 months), during which time you have:

- carried out corrective actions following any adverse audit findings
- carried out a management review to check its overall performance.

You are now in a position to look at the future. External recognition of the QMS is the logical next step.

Options for external recognition

Second-party audits (audits carried out by the customer)

If your organization wishes to obtain recognition of your QMS by your customers, you can inform them of the fact or invite them to audit your system. A positive outcome from this audit will help your organization be accepted on to the customer's 'preferred suppliers list' of organizations having a recognized QMS and meeting the requirements of ISO 9001:2000 for a specified scope of work. This recognition of your QMS may allow you to be considered for work that your organization has been previously debarred from. Indeed, there are organizations in the UK which will not put your company on to its 'tender list' for design or construction without a recognized QMS.

It may seem to be a strange thing to do, to invite a customer to audit your organization's QMS, but if you are confident about the operation of your system, then there should be no worry about being embarrassed by the findings of the audit.

Third-party audits (audits carried out by an external certification body)

Third-party certification is the process of obtaining external recognition of your organization's QMS by an independent certification body. There are literally dozens of such bodies offering

Use an accredited certification body if you want your QMS to be recognized by your clients.

this service. Some of these are sector-specific, but most have the background and experience to carry out external audits in many different types of organization.

If you opt for third-party certification, we recommend that you select an accredited certification body which is registered by the United Kingdom Accreditation Service (UKAS), the internationally recognized accreditation body. Don't be tempted to use a non-accredited body or your certificate may not be recognized by your clients.

Third-party certification

Why should you opt for third party recognition of your QMS? There are a number of reasons for choosing to go down this route and these are discussed below.

1 **Internal benefits**
   If your company is confident that the QMS is beneficial to its well-being, gives added value and acts as a tool for ongoing improvement, top management should consider third-party certification as a means of promoting the fact that they are a professional organization with a robust management system.

2 **Less auditing by your customers**
   When third-party certification came into being, one of its main selling points was that it would remove the need for customers to carry out their own second-party audits; instead, they could accept the audit reports of an independent organization.

   Before the advent of third-party certification many client organizations – mainly utilities such as the Ministry of Defence, British Rail and British Gas – carried out audits of their suppliers. This was to give them confidence that their suppliers/contractors were operating to their in-house QMS. This meant that many organizations in the construction and manufacturing industries were therefore subject to multiple audits by their clients, which was both time-consuming and very costly to both parties.

   Once third-party certification was established, and confidence grew in its effectiveness, most client organizations ceased to carry out second-party audits, on account of the time and cost, and instead put their faith in the audits carried out by recognized third-party certification bodies.

   If your company's QMS has been audited by such a body and has met the auditing standard (ISO 9001:2000), this recognition should theoretically be acceptable to all your customers and save them having to audit you themselves.

   However, there will always be some clients who insist on carrying out their own audits (maybe at an important stage of a contract) even if your organization has third-party certification. If this is the client's wish, it has to be accepted.

3 **The client demands it**

There are some client organizations that will not put your company's name on their tender list for certain types of work without evidence of third-party certification. This may seem quite restrictive, but the client is only saying that, if you operate a QMS, demonstrate that it is working in practice by having it audited by a recognized third-party certification body.

If you have a QMS it is important that your clients be aware of it.

This is one of the reasons why many companies have gone down the certification route.

4 **The marketing advantage**

A key reason for organizations choosing third-party certification is its usefulness as a marketing tool: *it gives visibility to your capability*. Your company may have an excellent QMS, which is maintained and audited on a regular basis but, without external recognition, it remains invisible.

If your system has been third party registered you can publish the fact by:
– printing the registration logo on your company's notepaper and any publicity/marketing information
– putting the logo on company vehicles and signage
– publishing the fact in tender submissions.

Your organization's name will also be published in a national Register of Assessed Organizations, which is like a telephone directory of certified organizations.

The third-party certification process

Selecting a certification body

As mentioned earlier, there are numerous certification bodies all purporting to offer you good service and provide you with a certificate at the end of the assessment process. Don't be misled by all the hype; select a certification body as you would any other supplier and go out to tender.

The recommended process is as follows:

1 Contact UKAS or use its website if you are unaware of the list of accredited certification bodies, or find out which certification bodies your competitors have used.

2 Contact three or four of the accredited certification bodies that you believe could provide the assessment service and would be recognized by your clients. *Remember one of the reasons for making this decision is for marketing purposes.*

3 Send out an invitation to tender, specifying your organization's scope of work, the number of employees and the number of locations involved. Alternatively, ring the certification body and request their standard proforma, which will require the necessary details to be supplied.

Stress the fact that you wish someone to visit you to give a presentation and that you expect to speak to someone who is knowledgeable about your business (for example, if you are an architectural practice, you would expect the representative to understand your needs).

4 On viewing the tender submission look at what the certification body has to offer in terms of:
   – track record in your industry
   – price
   – support service after certification.

5 Invite two or three of the bodies to give you a presentation of their proposal.

6 Arrange interviews to be attended by your quality manager, an appropriate director or partner and any others who have key involvement in the QMS.

7 At the interview the quality manager should give a short presentation outline of your QMS, the organizational structure and, very importantly, how many locations are involved.

8 Following the quality manager's presentation, interview the certification representative and establish the following:
   – Who would be the lead auditor carrying out the audit?
   – Is this lead auditor knowledgeable about your business? *(It is an advantage if this person is present at the interview, but this is not always possible.)*
   – Whether the lead auditor will be carrying out the six-monthly follow-up visits after the first audit to maintain continuity. *(Some third-party certification bodies don't always use the same auditor. This is not a good practice, as you would benefit from the lead auditor building up a knowledge of your organization and gaining a rapport with your staff.)*
   – Does the third-party presentation come across as being professional in its approach? Make sure you ask how they would plan and carry out the audit, how long will it take, when the audit might take place and what will happen after the audit. *(If the third-party certification body guarantees that your organization will be successful on the audit, think carefully. There is no guarantee that your organization will pass the audit first time without any corrective actions being identified, and that is how it should be. You don't want an auditor to accept your QMS if it does not fully meet the requirements of ISO 9001: 2000.*

9 Following the interviews with the certification bodies, choose the one best suited to your organization and credibility with your clients.

The third-party assessment process

The process that your organization will go through after placing a contract with the nominated body is generally as follows.

The lead auditor from the chosen certification body will:

- contact your organization (probably using the quality manager as the contact)
- arrange to review your QMS documentation to familiarize himself/herself with the scope and complexity of the organization
- discuss an audit programme covering:
  - the dates and times of the processes to be audited
  - the nominated staff to be available
  - an outline of what will be covered by the audit process
- send out the audit programme in advance of the audit date
- carry out the audit (maybe with other auditors) and prepare a report which may identify no problems or, in most cases, some corrective actions
- if no serious problems have been identified, recommend your organization for acceptance as a third-party registered company
- arrange for the certificate to be issued following the recommendation
- arrange six-monthly audit visits to monitor the ongoing effectiveness of the QMS.

System reviews

Throughout this book we have discussed many aspects relating to the QMS. Table 11.1 is essentially a reflection of the ISO 9001:2000 requirements expressed in the form of a series of questions, which we hope will prove useful in the following respects:

- as a cross-check for anyone setting up their QMS against the ISO 9001:2000 standard, to ensure that all points relevant to their organization have been covered
- to give an indication of the questions that a third-party certification body will be likely to ask when first examining your system
- as an indication to certain questions suitable for inclusion in audit checklists
- as a guide to possible KPIs.

	Yes/No	Comments
1 Scope		
• Are formal routines in place to establish applicable customer and regulatory requirements?		
• Are these understood and being applied properly?		
• Are provisions in place to establish and measure customer satisfaction?		
• Are such findings used effectively to promote the continuing improvement of the QMS?		
2 Normative reference		
• Is the QMS based on the current standard and/or revisions thereto?		
3 Terms and definitions		
• Is the terminology of the QMS consistent with the standard?		
4 Quality management system		
4.1 General requirements		
• Has the organization identified its key processes?		
• Is there an effective mechanism for equating these processes to known customer needs and adapting the processes as necessary to meet the same?		
• Are process sequences, interfaces and dependencies clearly defined?		
• Are the necessary resources to effectively carry out the processes, predetermined?		

Table 11.1 *A guideline to system reviews*

4 Quality management system (continued)	Yes/No	Comments
• Are the methods and criteria to ensure the effective operation and control of processes determined?		
• Is the necessary information to support the operation and monitoring of the processes in place?		
• Are all processes subject to continual measurement, monitoring and analysis such as to enable planned results to be achieved and the processes themselves improved?		
4.2 Documentation requirements		
• Is there a formal and controlled documented QMS? *(Note: procedures and documents may be in any form or type of medium.)*		
• Is the system such that it can readily and unambiguously be referenced, used and reviewed?		
4.2.2 Quality manual		
• Is there a controlled and up-to-date quality manual, which defines the scope of the QMS, its documented procedures (or clear reference thereto) and the sequence and interaction of the various processes in the QMS?		
4.2.3 Control of documents		
• Is there/are there formal procedures in place defining how documents required for the QMS are:		
– approved for adequacy prior to release?		
– reviewed, updated if necessary and re-approved?		
– given clear indication of their revision status?		
– made available at needed points of use?		
– maintained legible, identifiable and retrievable?		
• How are external originating documents and their distributions controlled?		
• How is the use of obsolete documents prevented?		

4.2.4 *Control of records*

- Is there a documented procedure (or procedures), which defines how such records are identified, compiled, stored/retained, protected, accessed periods of retention determined, reviewed and dispensations, authorized and implemented? *(Note: this may vary from process to process, be directly influenced by customer requirements, applicable legislation and so on.)*

5 **Management responsibility**

5.1 *Management commitment*

- Is it clear what top management's role in relation to the requirements of the QMS are, and what responsibilities are held by specific persons?

- Is there evidence of top management commitment to the understanding, development and improvement of the QMS?

  For example:

  – has the importance of meeting customer and regulatory requirements been emphasized to all members of the organization?

  – have a quality policy and quality objectives been defined?

  – are effective management reviews taking place?

  – are appropriate resources determined and being made available to implement, develop and improve the QMS?

5.2 *Customer focus*

- Are routines in place to determine the needs and expectancies of customers?

- Are they conveyed through a proper planned approach into identified resources, processes and controls?

Table 11.1 *Continued*

5 Management responsibility (continued)	Yes/No	Comments
• Are process results measured against customer expectations and satisfaction? • Are lessons learned, used to improve processes and performances? **5.3 Quality policy** • Is the quality policy appropriate to the purposes of the organization? • Does it include a commitment to meeting all requirements, to continual improvement and to providing a framework for establishing and reviewing quality objectives? • Has it been/is it being, properly conveyed and understood? • Is It reviewed for continuing suitability? **5.4 Planning** **5.4.1 Quality objectives** • Are measurable objectives, which are consistent with the quality policy being established at relevant functions and levels within the organization? • Do these include commitment to continual improvement? **5.4.2 Quality planning** • Are documented planned outputs being produced which identify the resources needed to satisfy the processes of the QMS and the continuing improvement of the system? • Does the planning of changes ensure the continuing integrity of the QMS during such changes? **5.5 Responsibility, authority and communication** **5.5.1 Responsibility and authority**		

- Are the functions, interrelationships, discrete responsibilities and authorities within the organization clearly defined and communicated?

5.5.2 *Management representative*

- Is it clear as to who in the organization ensures that:
  - the processes of the QMS are established and maintained?
  - the performance of the QMS and improvement needs are reported to top management?
  - awareness of customer requirements is promoted throughout the organization?

5.5.3 *Internal communication*

- Is a visible and effective communication system regarding the processes of the QMS and their effectiveness in place between the various levels and functions within the organization?

5.6 *Management review*

5.6.1 *General*

- Are reviews by top management formally planned and implemented?

- Do these include ensuring the continuing suitability, adequacy and effectiveness of the QMS and also of the quality policy and objectives?

5.6.2 *Review input*

- Do reviews include current performances and improvement opportunities as indicated by:
  - results of audits?
  - customer feedback?
  - process performance/conformance?
  - status of corrective and preventive action?
  - results of previous reviews?
  - potential changes to the QMS?

Table 11.1 *Continued*

		Yes/No	Comments
5	**Management responsibility (continued)**		
	5.6.3 *Review output*		
	• Do these include actions concerning:		
	– improvements to the QMS?		
	– improvement to products related to customer requirements?		
	– resource needs?		
	• Are records of reviews and actions emanating therefrom established and available?		
6	**Resource management**		
	6.1 *Provision of resources*		
	• Are resources available to maintain and improve the QMS?		
	6.2 *Human resources*		
	6.2.1 *General*		
	• Are procedures/routines in place/use to ensure that persons carrying out responsibilities as defined in the QMS are competent to do so by virtue of their education, training, skills and experience?		
	6.2.2 *Competence, awareness and training*		
	• Are the competency needs for personnel performing quality-related activities predetermined?		
	• Is training being provided as necessary?		
	• Are records of training, experiences and known competencies of persons kept and used to match people to activities?		
	• When training is provided, is it followed by an appropriate evaluation of its effectiveness?		

- Do personnel have an awareness of the relevance and importance of their activities in relation to the achievement of quality objectives?

6.3 *Infrastructure*

- Are appropriate workspace, equipment and service facilities provided?

6.4 *Work environment*

- Are the human and physical factors of the work environment properly identified, managed and conducive to achieving a conforming product?

7   Product realization

7.1 *Planning of product realization*

- Are processes required to achieve the product pre-identified, sequenced, resourced, implemented and controlled in accordance with properly documented planned measures (for example, quality plans)?

- Are records demonstrating process conformities and resulting product suitability complied with, maintained and available?

7.2 *Customer-related processes*

7.2.1 *Determination of requirements related to the product*

- Are clearly defined measures (such as formal contract review) in place to determine and clarify necessary, customer-specified requirements, as well as other relevant requirements, including regulatory and legal?

7.2.2 *Review of requirements related to the product*

- Are requirements being formally reviewed to ensure completeness of information, ability to resource activities and achieve required product result within laid-down expectancy timeframes and so on?

Table 11.1 *Continued*

7 Product realization (continued)	Yes/No	Comments

• Are persons responsible for such reviews clearly defined?
 	
 • Are any anomalies clarified with the customer, and formally confirmed, prior to any commitment being made to supply the product?
 	
 • Are records of reviews maintained?
 	
 7.2.3 *Customer communication*
 	
 • Are there identified arrangements in place for communicating with customers concerning such matters as:
 	
     – product information?
 	
     – enquiries, contracts or order handling and amendments thereto?
 	
     – product performance feedback including complaints?
 	
 • Is such information used, when appropriate, to improve product quality and/or process improvements?
 	
 7.3 *Design and/or development*
 	
 7.3.1 *Design and development planning*
 	
 • Are the various stages of the design and development processes defined/planned?
 	
 • Are the necessary review, verification and validation activities clearly defined?
 	
 • Are the interfaces between different groups involved in design and development activities identified and managed so as to ensure effective communication and clarity of responsibilities?
 	
 7.3.2 *Design and development inputs*
 	
 • Are all inputs necessary to achieve the design and development, clearly defined and documented, including typically (but not limited to) those pertaining to:		

    – functional and performance requirements?

    – applicable statutory and regulatory requirements?

    – feedback from previous designs?

- Have inputs been reviewed for adequacy and resolved in event of there being any ambiguity, incompleteness or conflict of requirements?

7.3.3 Design and development outputs

- Are outputs documented?
- Are they verifiable against inputs?
- Do they provide information to enable production, servicing, verification, commissioning, operation as appropriate?
- Do they define product characteristics essential to its safe and proper usage?
- Are there defined approaches for determining health and safety aspects?
- Are output documents approved prior to release?

7.3.4 Design and/or development review

- Are formal reviews being carried out at key stages of the design and/or development?
- Do these include continuing ability to meet requirements, identify problems, initiate remedial actions and verify their implementation?
- Are reviews carried out with the involvement of representatives of the functions involved with the design and development work in question?
- Are the results of reviews and any ensuing actions properly recorded?

Table 11.1 Continued

184

7 Product realization (continued)	Yes/No	Comments

7.3.5 Design and development verification
 	
• Are verification techniques which are to be deployed when they are appropriate fully and clearly defined in relevant procedure documents or similar?
 	
• Are these techniques understood and being properly deployed by people having appropriate skills, training, qualifications and so on?
 	
• Are the timely carrying out of planned verifications a subject of design reviews?
 	
• Are the results of verifications and any actions arising therefrom being properly recorded?
 	
7.3.6 Design and development validation
 	
• Are validations of design outputs planned, implemented, fed back, reviewed and used as a basis for future design thinking?
 	
• Are validation methods, experiences, results and so on and any actions arising therefrom being properly recorded?
 	
(Note: it is recognized that some validations may not become possible until long after completion of the design process – for example, until plant commissioning, operation or anticipated lifetime conditions have been met.)
 	
7.3.7 Control of design and development changes
 	
• Are changes subject to the same rigours as the original design and development work? For example, are they:
 	
  – clearly identified?
 	
  – documented?
 	
  – controlled?
 	
  – evaluated for effects on other products or parts?
 	
  – evaluated for health and safety implications?
 	
  – evaluated for verification/validation?		

– evaluated for pre-implementation approvals?

– properly recorded?

7.4 Purchasing

7.4.1 Purchasing process

- Does the organization evaluate and select its suppliers on their ability to meet the organization's requirements, typically considering such matters as:

  – technical ability?

  – financial stability?

  – resources?

  – the QMS and its application?

  – health and safety awareness and consideration?

  – existing track record?

- Are such evaluated suppliers listed and used selectively on the basis of their relevant known suitability?

- Are the ongoing performances of suppliers formally reviewed and appropriate actions taken when needed?

7.4.2 Purchasing information

- Do purchasing documents adequately define, as appropriate, requirements for approvals/qualification of the product, procedures, processes, equipment and personnel?

- Is it clear who decides on appropriate, requirements and on what basis?

- Is it clear what, if any, specific QMS requirements are to be met?

- Are purchasing documents subject to pre-release review to ensure the adequacy of the information contained therein?

Table 11.1 Continued

7 Product realization (continued)	Yes/No	Comments

7.4.3 Verification of purchased product
 	
•   Are appropriate verification activities being identified, defined and implemented and recorded?
 	
•   Where it is required that the organization or its customer perform verification activities at a supplier's premises, are such intended verification arrangements and methods of product release included in the purchasing information?
 	
7.5 Production and service provision
7.5.1 Control of production and service provision
 	
•   Are all stages of production and service operations controlled through:
 	
   –   information specifying product characteristics?
 	
   –   necessary procedures, instruction and so on?
 	
   –   the use of measuring and monitoring devices?
 	
   –   implemented monitoring activities?
 	
   –   defined processes for release, delivery and post-delivery activities?
 	
7.5.2 Validation of processes
 	
•   Has the organization identified those production and service processes where the resulting outputs cannot be verified by subsequent measuring and monitoring?
 	
•   Have such processes been validated to demonstrate their ability to achieve planned results?
 	
•   Are validation methods, personnel, equipments and required records clearly defined?
 	
• Do arrangements include for revalidation when necessary?		

7.5.3 Identification and traceability

- Where appropriate, are the means defined whereby the product is to be identified throughout production and service operations?

- Where traceability is a requirement, are measures being implemented to ensure and maintain its effectiveness?

- Is the 'status' of the product with respect to measuring and monitoring requirements known at all times?

7.5.4 Customer property

- Are procedures in place and being implemented to ensure the identification, verification, protection and maintenance of customer property (including intellectual property) provided for use or incorporation into the product?

- Is it defined how any loss, damage or unsuitability of customer property is to be recorded and reported to the customer?

7.5.5 Preservation of product

- Are measures in place to preserve the conformity of the product and its constituent parts throughout all internal processes and delivery?

7.6 Control of monitoring and measuring devices

- Are monitoring and measuring devices:
  - uniquely identified?
  - stored and handled so as not to allow damage or deterioration?
  - subject to planned calibration/adjustment at frequencies reflective of their usage or, if necessary, prior to each usage?

- Are the methods of calibration those which are correct for the type of gauge/instrument being checked?

Table 11.1 Continued

	Yes/No	Comments
7 Product realization (continued)		
• Is the calibration equipment itself of known accuracy at its time of use?		
• Are the results of calibrations, including dates, methods and results, being properly recorded?		
• If devices are found to be out of calibration, is the validity of previous results reassessed and appropriate corrective actions taken?		
• Is any software used for monitoring and measuring of specified requirements being validated prior to use?		
8 Measurement, analysis and improvement		
8.1 General		
• Are all monitoring and measuring requirements, to assure product conformity and improvement, established and defined, including their methodologies, timing and use of statistical techniques when deemed appropriate?		
8.2 Monitoring and measurement		
8.2.1 Customer satisfaction		
• Does the organization have in place procedures or similar to obtain feedback on customer satisfaction (or dissatisfaction) and using such information for improvement of the product and the QMS?		
8.2.2 Internal audit		
• Is there a planned audit programme in place showing audit intentions and implementations for a specific period?		
• Does the programme reflect the status and importance of activities and areas to be audited?		
• Does it indicate the intended scope of audits, their timing or frequency?		

- Are audits being carried out by persons other than those who carry out the activity being audited?
- Are audits carried out in accordance with a procedure which addresses:
  - their planning?
  - auditor conduct?
  - implementation?
  - reporting?
  - corrective action monitoring and reporting?
  - close-out?
- Are management taking proper and timely actions in response to audit findings?

8.2.3 *Monitoring and measurement of processes*

- Are those realization processes necessary to meet customer requirements being monitored/checked to confirm their continuing ability to satisfy intended purposes?

8.2.4 *Monitoring and measurement of product*

- Are measurements and checks being carried out at appropriate stages to verify that product requirements are being/have been met?
- Are evidences (for example, inspection reports) of conformity being produced and recorded?
- Is it clear that acceptance criteria have been/are being met, and that product releases are only taking place with proper authority?
- Are final releases only being made once all specified activities have been satisfactorily completed, unless otherwise approved by the customer?

Table 11.1 *Continued*

8	Measurement, analysis and improvement (continued)	Yes/No	Comments
	8.3 Control of non-conforming product		
	• Is there a procedure which addresses the identification and control of non-conforming product(s) to prevent their unintended use or delivery?		
	• Is non-conforming product that is subsequently rectified being subject to proper reverification to demonstrate conformity?		
	• Is it clear what actions are to be taken and by whom in the event of non-conforming product only being detected after delivery or use?		
	8.4 Analysis of data		
	• Is data concerning the ongoing effectiveness of the QMS being compiled with and used to identify scope for improvement to the same?		
	• Typical sources of information would be (but are not limited to):		
	– data generated by measuring and monitoring activities		
	– customer feedback		
	– conformance to customer requirements		
	– processes, product characteristics and trends		
	– suppliers.		
	• Are frequencies, responsibilities and methodologies for this requirement defined?		
	8.5 Improvement		
	8.5.1 Continual improvement		
	• Does the organization have a positive attitude and approaches towards the improvement of its QMS?		
	• Is this reflected through its quality policy, objectives and organizational culture?		

- Is full use made of information resulting from such sources as:
  - customer feedback?
  - data analysis?
  - audits?
  - corrective and preventive action?
  - management reviews?
  - those who work within the organization?

8.5.2 *Corrective action*

- Is there an effective procedure in operation which requires:
  - identification of non-conformances (including customer complaints)?
  - determination of root causes?
  - evaluation of the needs for actions to prevent reoccurrence?
  - determination and implementation of necessary corrective actions?
  - recording of results of actions taken?
  - reviews of their effectiveness?

8.5.3 *Preventive action*

- Is there/are there a documented procedure(s) requiring preconsideration of potential non-conformities in order to prevent their occurrence by initiating timely preventive action/measures?

- At a minimum, are the following covered within the above procedure:

Table 11.1 *Continued*

8	Measurement, analysis and improvement (continued)	Yes/No	Comments
	– requirements for identifying potential non-conformities and their causes?		
	– determining and ensuring the implementation of preventive action needed?		
	– recording results of action taken?		
	– review preventive action taken?		

Table 11.1 Concluded

Chapter **12**

Computers and Quality Management

You may be wondering why, throughout this book, no mention has yet been made about the use of computers, which are now commonplace throughout industry. During our careers both of us have worked as quality managers on some very large, technically complex projects which justified and enabled expenditure on some very advanced computer equipment and programs. During this period we became aware of a number of common factors, which led to problems either during or subsequent to the use of computers.

Although most of the following will be seen as obvious and common sense to many readers, we state them nevertheless; it can do no harm.

Choosing software

However marvellous a software package may seem to be, always take the following precautions:

Make sure you find out about the support available for any software before you purchase it.

1 Make sure that the software has been developed by a reliable source who will be around to provide support if and when needed and not by some genius dwelling in an ivory tower somewhere in academia who, when needed, is likely to have vanished without trace.

2 Ensure that the parameters of any software *fully* encompass the scope of any intended use.

3 Make sure that point 2 above can be demonstrated/proved by appropriate test applications and is fully backed up by the necessary documented instruction information. Certainly some years ago there was a considerable amount of software being sold, where the users were acting as guinea pigs and being used for debugging the product.

4 Ensure that users are given proper 'hands-on' training in advance of using any computer programs for real.

5 Ensure that, if regular pre-check 'calibration' type runs are needed, they *are* carried out.

6 Make sure that users fully appreciate the limitations of the programs they use.

7 For analytical type software – for example, that used for stress analysis and similar mathematical tasks – ensure that all printouts include not only the input and output data plus the name of the software package used, but also details of its particular version.

   If, at a later date, problems are encountered which can be traced back to a fault in the software, it may become very important to know what other work (such as structural design) had been done using that particular software version.

There are many software packages now on the market. Some appear to be very all-embracing and may in effect be significantly in excess of your actual needs and, as such, possibly an expensive option. When considering choices take the precaution of getting your in-house IT people to prepare the software specification and advise on choice.

The following precautions are also advised:

Maintain a list of who holds what software in the company. Apart from anything else, it will allow you to ensure you are complying with the licences you have bought.

- Maintain a register of all software owned by your organization, with a listed owner of each piece.
- Ensure that there is a system for preventing staff from using their own purchased software on the organization's PCs.
- Ensure that analytical software is supplied with details of verification and validation.
- Have 'version' controls of all software.
- Ensure that all PCs have 'virus checkers' installed.
- When software is being developed 'in-house' (including spreadsheets for those involved in data manipulation) ensure that verification and validation is carried out and that records are available.

Some applications

Throughout this book we have discussed many processes and types of document which lend themselves to computerization. The following are but a few examples.

Procedures and instructions

Although many organizations are still using, for preference, hard-copy information, there is nothing to prevent such documents being made available on a 'reader only' basis to those who need to use them.

It is the quality manager's responsibility to ensure that only the correct document issues are displayed, and this should be done at the same time as the master hard copy information is updated.

Printing these documents at the various computer stations is normally not allowed (unless safeguards are built into the system) as doing so could soon lead to out-of-date versions of documents in circulation around the workplace.

Problem and complaint reports

Often, when problems are found or complaints received concerning project work, they are dealt with as 'one-off' occurrences by the manager directly concerned. To a degree, this is understandable as the prime interests will almost certainly be to pacify the complainant and keep the project work flowing. The fact that identical problems may be being reported and dealt with on other projects may not be recognized. This is particularly likely if projects are being handled at more than one location such as different sites or different offices within an organization.

Once all problems are logged on to a database, their types and frequencies soon become apparent and have a greater impact by giving a wider picture of performance realities. The information produced allows problem situations to be prioritized (say, by number of occurrences, consequential costs and so on), proper attentions brought to bear, root causes determined and addressed, the most appropriate actions taken and their effectiveness monitored. We can both recall a typical example where a problem of being unable to obtain a particular material as specified was reported and dealt with by different recipients at several locations, something like 30 times over a 12-month period. Each occurrence incurred the costs of reviewing the problem, deciding on a solution, advising the complainant and subsequently modifying existing drawings, material lists and the like. With the kind of computerized system we have described the problem would have become apparent very early, an alternative material option specified, the problem overcome and a great deal of time, money and work flow disruption saved.

The calibration of inspection and test equipment

The quality manager or whoever is responsible for calibration will be assisted in managing this important function by a data display which allows the ready ability to access the following information:

- equipment type
- calibration source (for example, internal/external)
- calibration method (for example, as per makers' instructions)
- current calibration status
- last calibration date
- calibration frequency
- next calibration due date (with visual prompts)
- any special comments.

Standard clauses expressing quality-related requirements for inclusion in bid invitations and subsequent contracts

These could be put into a computer menu so that those clauses deemed appropriate for each particular package of contracted-out work could be selected in a form that is always consistently expressed. Typical of such clauses would be:

1   The bidder shall confirm that the subject work will be carried out in accordance with a QMS compatible with ISO 9001:2000 or the following parts thereof ...

2   The bidder shall submit with his bid a quality plan showing, at a minimum, the following in relation to the intended work programme:
    – intended organization and responsibility structure
    – methodology intended
    – applicable procedures to be applied
    – standards, regulations and so on to be worked to
    – records to be generated
    – liaison links to be used.

3   The bidder shall confirm his agreement to [organization name] carrying not more than ____ project-related audits during the work programme, such audits (if deemed necessary) to be carried out at times reasonable to both parties, provided that such timing does not jeopardize the effectiveness of the audit concerned.

Audit progressing

The advantages of having a visual display of the current state of auditing progress – that is, the planned audit schedule with details of audits intended, in progress, reported, corrective outcome completed – as an aid to the quality manager are very apparent.

In fact there are now software packages on the market which enable the management and distributions of much audit-related documentation, including those relating to:

- audit planning
- audit findings reporting
- corrective action reporting
- status reporting.

Access to such information can be particularly useful if 'Audit Performance' is one of your KPIs.

KPIs

These were discussed in Chapter 10. Again, a computerized database can be the ideal vehicle for inputting information and enabling its subsequent analysis to measure process effectiveness.

Typical specification requirements for a selection of software packages

1 Control and maintenance of the QMS

A typical package will have the following functionality:

- a database containing all documents which form the QMS
- hot links within procedures and instructions to all referenced documents such as standard forms
- a facility to amend documents and e-mail the drafts out for comment and, later, for approval and issue
- a capability of capturing all comments on the system
- visibility to all users of all stages from the draft to the approved version of the documents
- a facility for electronically archiving updated versions of documents
- a facility for printing hard copies from the system, suitably marked (for example, 'UNCONTROLLED WHEN PRINTED') to identify their status
- access to documents being controlled – for example, some documents may contain financial information, in which case a restriction may need to be placed on their access.

2 Control of suppliers

A typical software package would allow the following:

- a database of all suppliers
- access to standard quality statements to be used in purchasing documents
- provision to identify the status of all suppliers and change the status when necessary (on a limited access basis for this sensitive information)
- visit reports.

3 Records management

A typical software package would contain the following functions:

- a filing system for all project records
- a categorization system whereby the retention times for records can be identified when they are entered into the system
- a facility to remove records to an archive section
- a facility to recover records quickly from archives by searching on 'key words'
- a facility to hold confidential or documents with restricted access.

4 Maintenance

A typical software package would contain the following functions:

- a schedule of all equipment and suppliers of the equipment
- a list of all equipment out of service
- a list of contacts for spares
- a link to the maintenance instructions
- an ability to print out worksheets in advance of the maintenance being required, and sending out the request to carry out the planned maintenance
- an ability to capture all breakdown maintenance/unplanned work
- an ability to produce a variety of reports for top management
- a record of work completed and incomplete work
- a record of faults found and the corrective actions taken.

The *benefits* of the above software packages are as follows:

- Access to information can be given to all staff or a selected few
- The database can become the 'master record' rather than having numerous uncontrolled hard copies in circulation
- Everyone knows where the information is to be found rather than searching around for a 'controlled copy' of a document containing the information
- Accessing and amending information can be accomplished very rapidly
- Prompts can be sent out in a timely manner to remind staff to carry out various actions.

The disadvantages of using software packages are as follows:

People will believe information carried in your software programs, so make sure it is correct and up-to-date.

- There may not be a back-up if the system goes down, which causes delay and disruption to the project. People will tend to accept that the information on the system is correct. There has to be checks on information being put on the system, as in a paper-based system; otherwise, it will be a case of 'rubbish in – rubbish out'.
- Maintaining the system incurs a cost whether it is done in-house or by an external resource.
- There may be bugs or other problems in the system that don't show themselves during the verification and validation process.
- Off-the-shelf packages generally don't have the full functionality that your company desires, but purchasing bespoke software may prove very expensive.

Software problems and pitfalls

Purchasing software packages

Problem

Software that is purchased from an unreliable source by unqualified people and not installed properly, is unlikely to be maintained and can severely affect the company's performance.

Solution

- Use IT professionals to procure all software from recognized software suppliers who have been vetted.
- If you are having software developed (or customized) for your organization, ensure not only that there is a clear specification for the software but also that the software is verified and validated before use. This is particularly important with analytical software, which is used in the design process where mistakes could prove fatal – for example, in stress calculations in bridge design.
- Have a maintenance contract in place for the software, where required, to ensure that any problems can be resolved quickly.
- Within your own organization have a 'register of software' with a nominated owner for each piece of software. This will help to ensure that all updates to the software are issued to the owner, who in turn will control distribution of the new software to the users of the previous versions of the software within the organization in accordance with ISO 9001:2000, para . 4.2.3, 'Control of Documents'.
- Ensure that software is installed on PCs by IT professionals and not left to the users.
- Ensure that users are trained in the use of the software package.

Remember, most users need help to properly install software on their computer. Make sure it is available.

Use of spreadsheets

Problem

Some individuals are found to be using spreadsheets (which are manipulating data) without having the spreadsheet checked.

Solution

- Treat spreadsheets as a calculation. You would not issue a calculation to a client without first passing it through a checking and approval process.
- Check the spreadsheet by putting in known data where the answers have been checked by other means. Keep the checked example with that particular version of the spreadsheet.

- If an update is made to the spreadsheet, produce another test case to prove the changes are valid.

Believing all outputs from computers are correct

Problem

Some individuals are relying on computer outputs without carrying out basic checks.

Solution

Scanning documents (to minimize archive storage space) can sometimes lead to the corruption of the text – for example, subscripts and superscripts, Greek symbols and so on. It is therefore important to carry out a check on the new output before destroying the original document.

Documents can also be corrupted when they are transferred from one database to another database which are incompatible. Again, checking against the original is essential.

Use of e-mail

Problem

You assume that staff open e-mails promptly and, furthermore, read them.

Solution

If your QMS relies on people reading and responding to e-mails promptly, you have a problem.

We are living in the age of e-mail overload. If your QMS relies on staff responding to e-mails promptly (for example, responding to requests to comments on documents, responding to audit findings, responding to actions from meetings and so on), you will have problems.

Systems need to be managed and there has to be a personal touch. This means using the telephone, arranging meetings, using video, teleconferences or other means of personal contact.

E-mails have their place for confirming decisions, recording conversations and therefore providing a permanent record; they should not, however, be relied on as a means of managing a process without human intervention.

Chapter 13

The Future

You now have a QMS in place which you are using as a management tool to improve the effectiveness and efficiency of your organization. The following are subjects to consider as a way of building further on the benefits of operating your QMS.

Integrated management systems

What is an integrated management system and how does it differ from a quality management system (QMS) based on ISO 9001:2000?

The QMS is the organization's management system that is aimed at the achievement of results in relation to the quality policy and objectives. It satisfies the needs and expectations and requirements of stakeholders. On the other hand, an integrated management system looks at the parts of the business that have other objectives which complement the quality objectives. These related areas are typically environmental and occupational health and safety, but can include those related to the organization's growth and profitability.

An integrated management system therefore takes the various parts of an organization's management systems and brings them together into a single management system.

The benefits of the integrated approach

Many organizations still operate with separate parts to their management systems. Typically an organization could have:

- a QMS
- a safety management system including behavioural safety
- an environmental management system
- a human resource system
- a financial system.

Although organizations can operate quite successfully with the above separate systems, if they are moving to a 'process approach', as advocated by ISO 9001:2000, they should consider integrating their systems. Management systems share many common characteristics, and replacing the five systems listed above with a single management system would:

- eliminate conflicting responsibilities and interfaces
- reduce risks
- optimize working practices
- improve communications
- make it easier for staff to understand the management processes and probably reduce the amount of documentation
- create consistency of management systems
- help facilitate training and development
- balance conflicting objectives.

Integrating business and top management processes

The processes in the five management systems listed above include many complementary activities that could be linked together into single processes. For example, in the case of designing a bridge, the design process could include:

- typical quality-related design activities such as:
  - preparation, checking and verification of drawings
  - preparation, checking and verification of calculations
  - design reviews.

- typical safety-related activities such as:
  - complying with the CDM Regulations
  - carrying out risk assessments
  - operating a permit-to-work system.

- typical environmental activities such as:
  - carrying out environmental assessments
  - environmental audits.

All the above activities have an impact on the 'bridge design', and therefore if you drew up a process diagram for a design process it would include all of the above. It is therefore logical to integrate all the requirements into one process.

However, integration does not only apply to processes, it also takes into account all the other aspects of a management system, including top management processes.

As we have previously seen when reviewing ISO 9001:2000, top management have a key role in identifying systems and processes. Typically, these are:

- preparing the business plan, which includes goals and targets
- identifying policies
- identifying objectives and targets
- planning resources
- planning recruitment and ongoing training.

All the above can be incorporated in the integrated system as shown in Figure 13.1.

1	Business plan which includes objectives, goals and targets

2	Company mission statement or vision statement Company policies: • Quality • Environmental, Health and Safety • Financial • Human Resources • Security • IT • Standards • Legislation • Rules

3	Company organizational structure, including roles and responsibilities

4	Key business processes: for example, project management, resource management, construction management, business management, system management, environmental management, safety management.

5	Breakdown of key business processes into process activities which can be written as individual procedures or process flowsheets: for example, design, planning, IT, quantity surveying, document control and records, internal audits, contract management, purchasing and so on.

6	Site instructions	Standard forms	Guidance notes
7	Quality plans	Method statements	Risk assessments
8	Records and archives		

Figure 13.1 *A typical framework for an integrated management system*

Preparing an integrated management system

Do not consider preparing an integrated management system without having some mature management processes in place – in other words, processes which have been tried and tested.

It would also be difficult to try to document an integrated system in a new organization or one without both a safety manual and a quality manual, which are probably the two biggest contributors to the system.

If your organization meets the above criteria and you have decided to establish an integrated system, we suggest that the best route is as follows:

1 Identify the processes that are to be integrated (we suggest quality, safety and environmental).

2 Plan the process, including the objectives, goals and targets.

3 Produce a new mission statement and integrate the organization's policy statements into one.

4 Identify the organization's key management processes and prepare process diagrams to represent the inputs and outputs, taking account of the systems to be integrated. Also identify the owners of the key processes.

5 Modify the organization and responsibility information so that it acknowledges the integrated processes.

6 Follow the same route as compiling a quality manual (see Chapter 3).

The outcome should be a business-focused integrated management system which meets all your business requirements.

Behavioural safety

This is another subject that is now being given a higher profile within many organizations, and in some instances forming part of the integrated management system.

Organizations cannot lose sight of the fact that people's behaviour can have an adverse effect on the company's performance and therefore its profitability. Because of the poor accident record in the construction industry, we believe that a behavioural safety system should be part of the management system of all 'safety-conscious' companies.

What is behavioural safety and what is it not?

Behavioural safety is a way of reducing 'lost-time injuries' by analysing your current environment and applying proven performance management methods. There is evidence that the introduction of a behavioural safety culture into organizations has resulted in dramatic reductions in the number of lost-time and minor injuries.

One has only to look at the number of days lost through back injuries (caused by bad posture, incorrect lifting techniques, lifting too heavy a load and so on), to see what could be achieved if people changed their behaviours. Nevertheless, there are many critics of the behavioural safety concept, usually because they don't understand the underlying theory and feel it is a manipulative tool used by management to blame the workforce for poor safety practices.

Behavioural safety, however, is *not* about:

- disciplining people or having a blame culture
- trying to reduce accident rates based on unreliable data
- just focusing on reducing accident rates without encouraging safe behaviour.

So, what behavioural safety aspects are we therefore looking at?

First, you should be targeting the behaviours that cause accidents, not just the accidents themselves. To do this, you need to examine your company's existing 'accident/incident/near-miss database or accident/near-miss' books for data. Look at the frequency of specific behaviours involved and break these down by location. Use the 'Pareto' approach (that is, 20 per cent of unsafe behaviours will cause 80 per cent of the incidents reported) as a way of looking at the data and highlighting the real problems.

If you can identify unsafe behaviour and draw people's attention to it, you should reduce your accident risk.

The types of incidents or accidents and accompanying behaviours to look for are:

- eye strain through not conforming with advice or training on the use of display screen equipment
- car accidents as a result of falling asleep at the wheel, using a mobile phone and so forth
- injuries caused by falling over trip hazards such as electrical cables and items lying about on untidy building sites
- individuals cutting their fingers because of other people's thoughtlessness in putting items like broken glass bottles/sharp objects in wastebins designated for 'wastepaper only'
- breathing problems because of not reading the COSHH instructions before using paints, adhesives, cleaning agents and the like, or not complying with the regulations when using these materials.

Implementing a behavioural safety system

As with introducing a QMS everyone should be involved in introducing and implementing a behavioural safety system. As a guide, you should take the following steps:

1 Establish a consensus between top management and the workforce on the need for a safety culture.

2 Gain management commitment to safety and the involvement of the workforce at all stages.

3 Avoid introducing a 'blame culture', otherwise people will be reluctant to report accidents or near-misses and thus provide a learning tool so that improvements can be put in place.

4 Examine existing accidents/near-miss records and analyse them for behavioural safety issues (if they have been recorded in sufficient detail). Produce graphs, charts and diagrams illustrating trends.

5 In consultation with the workforce put together 'observation checklists' (to target accident-causing behaviours).

(Note: Although the misuse of personal protective equipment (PPE) may be the result of a behavioural safety issue, don't be tempted to add PPE to your checklist as this properly forms part of a safety audit. If, however, misuse of PPE is observed or any other unsafe practice, the observer should make a note and inform the appropriate safety person in the company.)

6   Involve staff in making observations in their own work areas and in completing the checklists.
(We recommend not recording people's names when making observations. People will react and be unwilling to cooperate with a behavioural safety system if they could be disciplined as a result.

7   Ask the observers who are completing checklists to record unsafe practices and not take the easy option of saying everything is all right and putting other people at risk, as such a strategy could backfire if there is an accident.

8   Remind observers that checklists are not audits of unsafe conditions; they are checklists of sample behaviours.

9   Make all staff aware that observations will be carried out in *their* work areas.

10 Encourage safe behaviour throughout the organization and provide behavioural safety training.

The benefits of operating a behavioural safety system

The benefits of such a system should be company wide:

- a safety culture should develop in the organization
- poor behaviours should be replaced by good behaviours as a result of regular feedback to the workforce on the benefits realized
- the accident record should be improved, which reduces time lost as a result of people's absence due to injury
- commitment to behavioural safety will become a habit that will not only help staff at work, but may extend to their behaviour both at home and in their leisure activities.

Chapter 14

Conclusions

In this book we have attempted to address, in a logical sequence and in easy-to-understand language, many aspects of quality management. Whether you belong to an organization that has still not embarked down the quality management road, are seeking to update your current QMS or are a student encountering the concepts of quality management for the first time, we hope that you will have found something of interest and help to you.

We have touched upon many things which can only benefit an organization, whether it has a formal QMS or not, such as teamworking, improvement initiatives, performance monitoring and so on. However, if your organization does have a QMS, or you are intending to set one up, hopefully we have demonstrated that it can be a major factor in relation to marketing your organization's capabilities, enhancing its image and competitiveness, managing its activities effectively and efficiently, monitoring its ongoing performance, continuing improvement, achieving your business objectives and satisfying your customers and clients.

One of the biggest challenges still faced by the construction industry is that concerning health and safety. Construction work, by its very nature, can present many hazards and associated risks. Although the CDM Regulations have attempted to bring closer attention to health and safety matters between the various parties involved in construction projects, words alone cannot bring about the improvements sought. As we have said earlier in this book, it is people who cause things to happen. We believe that real improvements in health and safety will only be achieved when all disciplines across a project really communicate about health and safety, with each genuinely trying to gain a greater awareness concerning the needs of, and constraints upon, others.

The 2003 HSE report and its findings concerning a regionalized survey into designers' awareness of their duties and obligations under the CDM Regulations emphasizes the validity of the point made above.

One step in the right direction is seen as that of integrating health and safety requirements into the organization's QMS, thus making them more visible, less likely to be overlooked or discounted, whilst simultaneously reminding people of their importance.

A further step, we believe, would be the provision of more tailored designer training in designing for safety in construction, ideally including an insight into the contractor's point of view, whose site-experienced approach to dealing with a risk situation may differ significantly from that of the designer. Such training is not seen as difficult to organize and its benefits, we believe, could be very significant indeed.

Brian and Peter

Brian Thorpe C.Eng, MIMechE, M.IEE, MIE.D, FIQA

Brian has had extensive experience at senior management level in engineering design, project management, sales and marketing, manufacturing and consultancy including more than 25 years in quality management.

He has worked within a wide range of British industries including aerospace, nuclear energy, food, textiles, waste management and construction.

He is an author and presenter of numerous training courses relating to a wide range of quality management subjects, including many relating to the construction industry, and has been a regular speaker on quality matters both within the UK and abroad. He has held the position of quality manager with several UK organizations and has been responsible for the application of quality management on some of the largest high-technology projects in Europe.

For six years he was head of one of the country's leading quality management consultancies, which was itself based within a construction engineering organization. Brian has helped numerous organizations of all types and sizes to develop 'right for them' quality management systems and gain third-party certification.

He was a co-author of the two previous versions of this book and is also the author of the book *Addressing CDM Regulations through Quality Management Systems* (Aldershot: Gower, 1999), besides being the writer of many published articles on different aspects of quality management. For twelve years he was a lead assessor of quality management systems. Now retired from full-time work activities, Brian continues to provide support to others, purely on a 'request for help' basis, where he feels qualified to do so.

Peter Sumner MCIM, MIQA, DMS

Peter has had a lifelong background in the engineering industry and spent many years in design, prior to moving into quality management in the late 1970s.

During the past 25 years he has worked both within the UK and abroad, helping numerous organizations to introduce quality management systems.

In conjunction with Brian, he has developed and run numerous training courses on different aspects of quality management, including many relating to construction activities.

He has had extensive experience in the application of quality management across major engineering projects.

Peter currently runs his own quality management consultancy specializing in integrated management systems. He additionally offers his services as planning supervisor and, as a registered lead assessor, carries out independent audits or behalf of his clients. He has also acted as quality manager for several companies including some within the construction industry. Peter was a co-author of the first and second edition of the book, *Quality Assurance in Construction* (Aldershot: Gower, 1996).

We all need skills. Just look around.

Take a look around any construction site in the UK and you'll find highly skilled people; many individuals from the 35,000 people per annum, both Adults and New Entrants (apprentices) who we have trained to enhance not only their careers, but also the companies they work for.

Look closer at any one of our four superb college sites across the UK, in Birmingham, Glasgow, Erith or Bircham Newton in Norfolk and you'll see the best instructors and the best facilities. We can even offer this same excellent standard of training at your own premises or a local training venue.

As the UK's leading construction skills training suppliers, we offer not only the best training, we also give you free professional advice on finding the right training, assistance in sourcing grant aid, building customized training courses and ultimately delivering the skills that you'll need.

If you're looking for, quite simply, the best construction skills training, look no further than the National Construction College and you'll see a way to a great future in the Construction Industry.

**For high quality yet cost effective
training, call us now on:
08475 336666
for Adult training
01485 577669
for Apprentice training**

Investors in People, ISO 9001:2000 and City and Guilds accredited.

National Construction College

Titles in the Leading Construction Series

Project Management in Construction
Dennis Lock
Hardback   208 pages   0 566 08612 3

Quality Management in Construction
Brian Thorpe and Peter Sumner
Hardback   234 pages   0 566 08614 X

Improving People Performance in Construction
David Cooper
Hardback   184 pages   0 566 08617 4

Winning New Business in Construction
Terry Gillen
Hardback   c. 130 pages   0 566 08615 8

For more details of these books or new titles in the series visit www.gowerpub.com or contact our sales department:

Sales Department, Gower Publishing Limited, Gower House, Croft Road, Aldershot, Hants, GU11 3HR, UK. Tel: +44 (0)1252 331551 e-mail: info@gowerpub.com